The Emperor's Virtual Clothes

The Emperor's Virtual Clothes

The Naked Truth about Internet Culture

by Dinty W. Moore

Algonquin Books of Chapel Hill   **1995**

Published by
Algonquin Books of Chapel Hill
Post Office Box 2225
Chapel Hill, North Carolina 27515-2225

a division of
Workman Publishing
708 Broadway
New York, New York 10003

Printed in the United States of America.
Printed simultaneously in Canada by Thomas Allen & Son Limited.
Design by Barbara E. Williams.

Library of Congress Cataloging-in-Publication Data
Moore, Dinty W., 1955–

The emperor's virtual clothes : the naked truth about Internet
culture / by Dinty W. Moore.

p. cm.
ISBN 1-56512-096-5

1. Information superhighway—Social aspects. 2. Internet
(Computer network)—Social aspects. 3. Computer networks—
Social aspects. I. Title.
HE7568.M66   1995
303.48'33—dc20   95–21180
                                                      CIP

10 9 8 7 6 5 4 3 2 1
First Edition

For Renita Marie Romasco

Acknowledgments

My deepest gratitude to the many individuals who so willingly shared their experiences, both on and off the Net. Without them, there would be no book. I would also like to thank Kjell Meling and Pennsylvania State University for their support, Bruce Weigl for his encouragement, George Romasco for lending me my first computer, and Robert Rubin for his trust in my ability to enter the electronic woods and not get hopelessly lost.

Since most of what we are told about new technology comes from its proponents, be deeply skeptical of all claims.

—Jerry Mander, *In the Absence of the Sacred*

Everybody gets so much information all day long that they lose their common sense.

—Gertrude Stein

Contents

INTO THE ELECTRONIC WOODS

Or, What's the Big Deal, Anyway?

The National Mall sweltered, the humidity was impenetrable, and thunderstorms boomed and rolled just across the Potomac, so I shuffled into line behind an unruly swarm of overheated, overstimulated, overspent tourists heading for the Smithsonian's National Museum of American History. It was air-conditioned, it was free, they had Archie Bunker's chair.

I had long wanted to see that chair and maybe get a quick glance at Edgar Bergen's wooden pal Charlie, but once inside the museum, I instead found my eye drawn to a big blue sign:

Information Age: People, Information & Technology

I was in our nation's capital for a reason, pursuing some sensible explanation for the sudden explosion of interest and speculation about the so-called Information Superhighway. Why, I wanted to know, was everyone from Vice President Al Gore on down so sure this would change the world? Why was every magazine, newspaper, and television chat show suddenly treating the

Internet as if it were the Second Coming of some electronic messiah? What was the big deal, anyway?

Moments before, in the Gerald R. Ford House Office Building, I had listened politely as eager congressional staffers stuffed my brain full of utopian visions of democracy unleashed. They tried to explain, held up statistics, but the picture was far from clear. I was reaching a point where the more I knew, the less I understood.

To clear my head, I'd hoped to take a relaxing journey through the Golden Age of Television; but instead duty called: the Age of Information was beckoning to me again, with additional info. I took a deep, long breath and was directed by the sign into a hallway lined with glass cases.

At the exhibit's start, I saw a crude machine: Samuel F. B. Morse's telegraph, "the beginning of instantaneous communication in America." From there, the corridor led me rapidly past old telephone poles, a mannequin family crowded around an enormous art deco radio, a blurry early television with a screen the size of a small watermelon, and finally into the Computer Age, with its ponderous mainframes, vacuum tubes, and banks of tangled wires.

To my considerable disappointment, though, the much-heralded Internet was represented by a single computer terminal, and that terminal was stuck under a glass box. Did the Smithsonian know something I didn't? Was the Information Superhighway so dangerous? I noted that the computer's keyboard had been removed as well, in case the glass should break.

A small white exhibit card underneath the imprisoned computer promised this:

By using the telephone to connect their home computers to those of information companies, people can shop for groceries, exchange messages, pay bills, move money between bank accounts, and play computer games.

Dangerous? Hardly. Not even revolutionary. The Smithsonian's display made the Internet sound like nothing more than a cross between the Home Shopping Network and Nintendo. I stared at the blinking screen and thought, for the moment at least, that perhaps I had found the truth. Would the Information Superhighway be nothing more than a glorified ATM machine with laser blasters? Was it destined to become yet one more diabolical method by which retail conglomerates moved the point of sale a step closer to our wallets? Was the rest just so much hype?

On that oppressive July afternoon, it seemed I was the only person in the Smithsonian who really cared. The crowds of tourists ignored the glass box, jamming themselves instead around a nearby exhibit on high-definition television. The sleek screen displayed a pair of cumbersome Japanese sumo wrestlers facing off on a blue mat. As the wrestlers tossed themselves to and fro like a pair of shaved bears, the tourists grinned, pointed, and nodded their complete approval. The only information revolution they wanted, it would seem, was one with a really clear picture, a really big screen, and really big men trying to knock one another down.

The Information Superhighway. The Internet. The new frontier that science fiction writer William Gibson dubbed cyberspace.

Whatever you call the network of networks that links upward of 35 million computer users worldwide, it is certainly bigger than a sumo wrestler, bigger than an arena full of sumos. Estimates are that someone new plugs into the Internet on the average of every ten minutes, and that dizzying rate of growth is itself expected to increase. In fact, based on current growth rates, some have estimated that every person on the planet will be "networked" by the year 2003. Soon, they say, we will all be hooked in, turned on, electronically joined at the hip.

But what will it mean?

If you believe the proponents, the zealots, those who not only love computers but see them as mankind's salvation, this amazing phenomenon will in the very near future transform our culture, alter the political process, rearrange the balance of world power, and change the way we think, the way we learn, the way we fall in love. Experts, armed with bits of bright, shiny jargon, assert in no uncertain terms that the Internet will change absolutely everything, right down to the fundamental ways in which we relate as human beings.

On the other hand, oracles of doom see nothing but evil: international computer sabotage, government agents snooping into every aspect of our lives, anti-government anarchists exchanging plans for making bombs, pornography in every home, a world filled with anemic drones laboring away at sterile keyboards, never seeing the light of day, never tossing a Frisbee to their dog. The Internet, it seems, is the final nail in mankind's coffin, a glowing nail, sharp as a tack but evil through and through.

So, who is right? Which will it be?

I think, if you will excuse my using technical terminology here, that both sides are full of hooey.

When it comes to the Information Superhighway, this much is clear: one side's overstatement rapidly drowns out the other side's hyperbole, and that hyperbole is itself instantaneously suffocated under a smothering layer of gross media exaggeration. No one really knows, in other words. They are all just guessing.

To counter this, to find something vaguely resembling an actual fact, I undertook my own investigation. The experts, you see, are already so smitten with technology that they can hardly be objective. I, on the other hand, am not smitten in the least. My technologically current friends inform me regularly, in fact, that the computer I own is dangerously out of date. It won't run the newest, hottest software. It runs the old software rather slowly. The screen displays just two colors: orange on black. No sound, no graphics. No bells, no whistles.

I am not a computer programmer, a technician, or an engineer. Instead, I'm a writer who's paid to teach college students to write stories, novels, poems, and other similarly impractical things. I am a skeptic by nature, and I pride myself on knowing simple deceit, or pure embellishment, when I see it.

When I run across a new technology, I want that technology to improve my life, make it more efficient. What I specifically *don't* want is any technology, no matter how new or how clever, that makes an easy task five times more complex, or that leaves me feeling like some Jed Clampett hillbilly in a dizzying, digital, difficult high-tech Beverly Hills.

In researching this book, I hoped to learn exactly how the coming Information Superhighway might affect people like myself: the technologically innocent, the everyday souls who use a phone, perhaps a computer, maybe even a fax machine at work, but don't particularly care how those machines are assembled, who builds them, or how many gigabytes of data can fit on the head of a pin.

Crystal balls are fun but not accurate. Instead of hopeful predictions, in lieu of wild speculation, I focused on the so-called Information Superhighway as it exists in early 1995, with at least its preliminary roadways in place. If 35 million users are already hooked into computer networks such as the Internet, what are they doing there, what interesting uses have they found, and are any of these interesting uses actually useful?

The writer Henry David Thoreau once tried to make sense of a rapidly changing world by venturing into the Massachusetts woods near Walden Pond and living there awhile. "I wanted to ... drive life into a corner," he wrote, "and reduce it to its lowest terms, and, if it proved to be mean, why then to get the whole and genuine meanness of it, and publish its meanness to the world; or if it were sublime, to know it by experience, and be able to give a true account of it." He did this, he said, because he saw that most men were "in a strange uncertainty," that they were unsure whether life itself was "of the devil or of God."

Instead of retreating *from* a changing world, I retreated *into* it, venturing onto the new digital footpath, immersing myself for a full year in the electronic woods. My reasons were much the same as Thoreau's—I wanted to reduce this new world to something understandable, to learn if the new electronic culture was mean or sublime, of the devil or of God.

Thoreau prized simplicity, and I tried to keep my questions simple as well. Who was using it? What were they using it for? Were they using it for anything useful?

I tried, too, to keep the answers simple, though that was no easy task. The woods I traveled were as full of jargon as Thoreau's woods were full of old, dry leaves. Still, I attempted to rake the jargon into a pile whenever possible, and to set the pile aflame, to translate the strange language of computer networks into a language all of us can understand. If it doesn't make sense in simple language, I told myself, don't trust it.

At the Smithsonian that day, printed on the wall behind the telegraph, I saw a quote from Samuel F. B. Morse. "I see no reason," he predicted in 1832, "why intelligence might not be instantaneously transmitted by electricity to any distance."

Well, almost everyone knows by now that all sorts of information can be instantaneously transmitted on this highway of computers. Words, yes. Pictures, surely. Dirty pictures? We'll cover that in a later chapter.

But what about "intelligence," as Morse promises? Is intelligence being instantaneously transmitted, or just meaningless drivel? Is there, in fact, any intelligent life in cyberspace?

That was my quest, to follow that star, no matter how hopeless, no matter how many hours of Internet access time I logged onto my credit card. I ventured deep into the electronic woods with little more than the clothes on my back and my cranky, outdated, embarrassingly sluggish home computer, and I chronicled what I found, who I met, and the amazing and/or ridiculous things they were doing; and, yes, I came out alive, relatively intact, and with my own perspective on the Big Question:

Is the electronic culture revolutionary, transformational, dazzling, and will it change our lives? Is it the Next Big Thing?

Or is it just the Emperor's New Clothes?

chapter one

HOW DO WE GET ON?

A Nontechnical Technical Explanation

Here is the truth: there is no Information Superhighway, though it pretty much already exists.

Consider that a Zen koan.

In point of fact, Information Superhighway is just a bureaucrat's buzz phrase. No one is even sure who first used it, though many people have accused Vice President Al Gore. The term Information Superhighway is applied with stunning abandon these days, often erroneously, to mean just about anything linked to a wire—your telephone, your cable television, your doorbell. This is part of the confusion many people face, and surely part of their apprehension.

Moreover, the term Information Superhighway is meant to sound exciting and fast, but to many it seems distressingly ominous, like a place the average man might get run over, and seriously hurt.

There is no Superhighway, never was, and there may or may not ever be one. What exists is something else, a vast global network of computers sending messages back and forth. Some call

1

this network the Internet, though that is not entirely accurate either. The Internet is only a part of the whole. Beyond the Internet, there are commercial services such as CompuServe, America Online, Prodigy, and others, which are, to varying degrees, linked "on-line" to the Internet. Beyond those, there are thousands of smaller entities, often called BBSs (Bulletin Board Systems), some of which are linked to the Internet, and some of which are not. Sound confusing? It is.

Many people just say Internet and leave it at that, since the Internet is certainly the area where most of the activity takes place. Others have begun to use an abbreviation of sorts, "the Net," to indicate the whole shebang. Many people just throw up their hands.

Even the experts disagree on terminology, I'm afraid, but here is what you really need to know:

A network is two or more computers electronically connected so that they can communicate back and forth. The Internet is made up of an estimated twenty thousand of these computer networks, all networked together, mostly by phone line, linking millions of individual computers and resulting in one big, unruly network of networks.

Think for a moment of an enormous lace doily, like the one on the back of my Aunt Philomena's Victorian sofa, but this one is draped across the planet, with each knot representing a different computer. Now imagine that the lace doily conceals a billion tiny wires, and these wires can send words or pictures back and forth between the knots at breakneck speed, almost as fast as we can type them in.

The Net is a little like a gigantic lace doily that glows. The Net is what most people mean when they say Information Super-highway. The Net is the home of the electronic culture, if such a thing exists. The Net is already in place, and working.

But then there are the futurists, those people who can't stop living for tomorrow. Having perhaps read that little white card in the Smithsonian, the futurists envision someday linking up these communicating computers to your cable television wires, adding connections to the ATM programs at your bank, splicing in the major airline reservation systems and all those pesky shop-at-home catalog companies, and eventually tying all of this into your electronic garage-door opener. *That* would require a very large and intricate doily indeed, and whether it will ever really happen is anybody's guess, and many a person's nightmare.

So who is using this Net, and what are they doing?

The Internet, this amazing new thing, is actually over twenty-five years old. It began as something called ARPANET and was for quite some time the exclusive domain of research scientists, most of them housed in big universities, many of them working for the Department of Defense. The network grew, by leaps and bounds, eventually going overseas, pulling in more and more scientists, then graduate students, and eventually just plain people.

Today, many of these same researchers are still around, still on the networks, as are their colleagues and many of their former students. If you have a technical question about software or physics or molecular biology, the Internet is still a very good place to ask it.

But the balance is shifting.

Mike Miskulin, a regular contributor to an electronic discussion group focusing on physics, notes that "the average discussion has plummeted. Where at one time you could find a number of 'serious' discussions, now [the physics group] is a haven for crackpots and endless [conversations] on faster-than-light travel."

Everyday folks with plebian interests are more the norm now. Part of this is due to the popularity of commercial "access providers" such as America Online and CompuServe—these firms are doing for the Net what McDonald's did for the cheeseburger. Part of it is simply word of mouth—access to the Net can be interesting, and it can be fun. The number of current Internet users is estimated to be jumping fast—to 20 million, or 30 million, or 40 million—as with any worthwhile statistic, no one can really agree.

What everyone does agree on is that the number of users is rocketing skyward. More and more newcomers are using the Internet to find an enormous amount of information, some of that information crucial, technical, or fascinating, much of it just silly. They look at pictures on their computers, sometimes pictures of comets crashing into distant planets, oftentimes pictures of distant women without any clothes. They join other computer users with similar interests—gardening, ice cream, destroying the earth—and then trade messages about that topic. They send one another electronic letters, some angry, some friendly, some short, some long.

The Internet and the related networks that make up the greater Net are used for just about everything under the sun—

from mere socializing to support and therapy, from chat about hobbies to serious research, from commerce to crime. What is done on the Internet simply mirrors what is done off the Internet, the only difference being that on the Internet it all happens electronically, and very, very fast.

How do I get on?

Shouldn't you finish this book first, see if you really *want* to get on?

Well, I was impatient, too, fighting my way onto the Internet before I was even sure how to spell it. I don't do scientific research, so that was certainly not my reason. Mainly, I was curious. It seemed more and more people were talking about this Net thing, and I didn't want to be the one person who got left behind.

So I bought a modem (a piece of computer equipment that I really don't understand) and held my breath as I hooked the modem into my antiquated computer. I plugged a cord from my modem into my phone jack, then held my breath again. All in all, it took me about a day and a half before I could get it to work.

I am among the lucky ones actually, because I get free Internet access through the university where I teach. You see, to use the Internet, your own computer has to be physically connected up somehow—usually over the telephone. It then has to call a place that lets you hook into the Internet directly, or through a "host" computer—some other computer somewhere that is already tied in—and that computer connects you to the Net.

Think of the host computer as an old-fashioned switchboard operator maybe, the one who used to patch through your call.

Frankly, the way it all works gets dull and technical, but here is the bottom line: you need to find someone who will let you hook on, and there are numerous ways to do this.

You could get a university account simply by going back to college. Almost every college and university of any size is linked to the Internet now, and increasingly they are linking up all their students. Depending on the tuition, this might be an expensive option, but you would also get to skip classes and drink enormous quantities of beer.

Short of that, however, and assuming you don't work in a big government office, or at Hewlett-Packard, IBM, or some other high-tech firm with a big computer and free access for all its employees, you will probably need to look for an Internet "access provider."

These access providers come in all different sizes and shapes. Your main choice will be between one of the major national services, such as America Online, Prodigy, CompuServe, or Delphi, or one of a host of usually local, smaller, lower-cost access providers. They offer a range of services, and differing levels of Internet access, and this all changes from month to month, so your best bet is to ask around.

For now, know that the big difference between the major national services and the low-cost, no-frills local providers is often the "interface"—you will have a choice between a "command-line interface" and a "GUI." (GUI is pronounced "gooey," because it is sweet and probably addictive; it is short for Graphic User Interface, just one of an approximate 216 million intimidating bits of technical language invented by those who program computers for a living—one more reason why computer dweebs can't get dates.) Translated for the common man, *GUI* and *command-line interface* are just fancy names for "the stuff you see on your screen."

After you connect with a local, low-cost access provider, for instance, you might see this:

===>

This is a command line. In other words, you will need to type a "command." (Hint: either type "menu" or "help," or shut off the machine and go get coffee.)

The major on-line services such as Prodigy and CompuServe, on the other hand, are quite different. They are *not* the Internet, strictly speaking; they are simply companies with big computers that are willing, for a fee, to connect you *to* the Internet, or to one of their other fee-based information features—many of which are like the Internet, only tamer. The big commercial providers will even send you free software and information, and give you free time to fool around on-line (a tactic they learned from drug dealers maybe?). They are very popular and profitable. When you connect with most of these firms, instead of a vague command line, you will see pictures on your computer screen, and these pictures, known as icons, will have labels like "Go Shopping," or "Go Read Sports News," or "Go to Jail, Go Directly to Jail, Do Not Pass 'Go,' Send Us $200." All you have to do is point your computer mouse at one of these icons, click a button, and wait for things to start happening.

And if even that seems too difficult, the newest trend in GUIs is little pictures. Apple's e-World, for instance, presents pictures of buildings (a bank, a shopping mall, an "Arts & Leisure Pavilion"), and you can just point at the picture. This will allow people who can't even read to use the Internet, though what they will do when they get there is entirely unclear. (And a bit frightening.)

I know, I know, it all sounds daunting. The jargon is thick and new, the hardware and software commands can be confusing, no one agrees whether it is better to pay one of the big guys, save money with one of the small guys, or stay on the sofa and just watch television. The good news, though, is that the people who do know how to hook up modems, how to make those modems dial up a big computer, how to wade through the command lines and the GUIs and actually find the Internet, tend to be very eager to show other people. Perhaps your brother-in-law knows all about it and will hook you up for a beer and a sandwich? If that fails, buy one of the many technical guides in your bookstore's computer section. There are a kazillion of them, and probably one that is specifically written for your computer and your situation.

Yes, but if I do get on, can I ever get off?

This is a deliciously ambiguous question, given the extent to which sexual and erotic issues are discussed on the Internet, but the simple answer, for the moment, is "of course." All you have to do is reach along the side of your computer, find the big red power button, and push it down. That gets you out of there very fast.

In the future, the answer may become more fuzzy. Right now,

the Internet is a habit and habitat of choice. Ten years from now, however, you may ultimately need to be connected to do your banking, to watch the five hundred new channels of future television, or to do your job. Just as the average employer would probably give you one of those funny sidelong glances right now if you announced that you didn't have a telephone, it may be true in the very near future that not having Information Superhighway wires running right into your living room will be akin to living like Fred Flintstone.

The pressure will likely be on you to be wired and if you believe the doomsayers, those wires will be linked directly to major marketing firms and the government. They will know what you read, when you read it, what you watch and how often, what you buy and what you spend for it, to whom you send electronic mail, when you last visited a doctor, your college grades, and perhaps what is in the electronic letters you send. This future scenario worries libertarians, privacy activists, and paranoids a great deal.

It would probably worry Thoreau.

As for myself, I don't really know what the future holds (though I would like a three-week vacation). What I do know is that, whatever happens, the future is likely to be very interesting. And for many people, including those you are about to meet, it is already here.

chapter two

IN SEARCH OF USEFUL USES

The Weird, Wired World of Usenet

Well, here is something useful:

On my computer one morning, I learned the proper way to elevate a cantaloupe. You go to the grocery store, buy some strawberries, eat them, take the green plastic basket that the strawberries came in out to the garden and turn the basket upside down, then plop the growing cantaloupe right on top of it.

This information is not so earth-shattering—unless the cantaloupes in your garden are rotting from the bottom up.

Mine were, but they aren't anymore.

My brain might be rotting from the bottom up, however, because I've spent the last twelve months on my computer reading messages, asking hundreds of questions, offering hundreds of answers, being electronically insulted, electronically insulting others, trading my thoughts and opinions on the strangest topics with millions of people I have never met. I have been visiting the wired world of Usenet.

Usenet is one of the most popular aspects of the Net, the area that many newcomers finds themselves drawn to first. What is it?

Well, my grocery store has a series of bulletin boards along one wall just past the checkout line, and customers are encouraged to post flyers and notices on these boards. The boards are divided by topic, along the lines of "items for sale," "social events," "items wanted," and "services offered." Shoppers bring their own index cards and thumbtacks, and post just about any message they want.

Usenet, in essence, is just like that: a big, electronic bulletin board. Or, more accurately, it's a series of bulletin boards, divided by topic. At last count, there were over ten thousand topics represented. There are no thumbtacks, of course—you can only post notices and read notices on these bulletin boards by using your computer.

And Usenet goes a bit beyond the metaphor. On a real bulletin board, like the one at my grocery store, people merely read your notice, maybe jot down a phone number, then wander away. On an electronic bulletin board, or on one of the thousands of Usenet "newsgroups" available through the Internet, people read your notice, and then can type a reply into their computer and send that reply through the electronic lace doily to hang on the newsgroup wall right next to your notice, and hundreds or thousands of other people can read that, too, and maybe write their own reply.

How does it happen? This gets technical. The big "host" computers essentially cooperate to store and forward the thousands upon thousands of individual Usenet messages—there is no center to this doily, you see, just lots and lots of knots and wires.

Here's an example of Usenet at work:

Let's imagine that you become curious to know why your cat

Cheetah sleeps on the bathroom floor next to the toilet brush. You can type the question into your computer on Monday evening, use your Internet access to "post" this question to a Usenet newsgroup dedicated to the discussion of cats, then go to bed (but hopefully not near Cheetah). While you sleep, hundreds of wired cat lovers will see your question on their home computers, deliberate, and offer advice. (My suggestion: get a new cat.) On Tuesday morning, turn on your computer, press the keys that take you to the cats newsgroup, and read the answers.

Presto.

Cats are a big topic on the Net, as are kids, computers, music, movies, and politics. There are new groups being created every day, and the list of topics is truly exhaustive: abortion, anagrams, amazon women, backrubs, banjos, Chinese computing, coupons, devil bunnies, drugs, genealogy, hamsters, hot rods, ketchup, motorcycles, pantyhose, religion, romance, satanism. Name any subject that interests you and chances are very, very good that some group on Usenet is discussing it right now. Chances are even better that they disagree.

Best estimates by computer magazines put the total number of people using these Usenet forums at more than 7 million, and this number is also spiraling upward.

But what is really useful about Usenet?

Well that depends on who you are, and on your interests.

One of the first things you will notice within the Usenet portion of the burgeoning Net is that there are different groups of groups. Each newsgroup has a name, and that name is divided by dots (so.the.computer.will.know.that.it.all.goes.together.)

The beginning of the name tells you what kind of group you are reading. For instance, the group comp.sys.ibm starts with "comp," which simply means that it is one of many groups that discuss computers and computing (in this case, IBM systems). If a group begins with the letters "sci," look for a discussion of some scientific discipline or controversy, as in sci.archeology, sci.bio.evolution, or sci.physics.plasma.

By now, of course, most people joining Usenet for the first time are not computer technicians or scientists. You will find many of the newcomers in the "rec" groups—short for recreational (like rec.pets.cats, rec.movie.reviews, or rec.skydiving). I needed a chicken curry recipe one night, posted a request on rec.food.recipes, and within twenty minutes some nice fellow in Ireland sent me three. I've seen people give advice on wedding photographers, sports equipment, prescription medicines, and muffler repair. Some discussion is technical, much of it is gossipy. You don't always know who is giving the advice, so be wary, but there is always plenty of advice from which to choose.

Other groups of groups include "news," "soc," "talk," "misc," "alt," and a growing number of smaller groupings, many of them regional. A number of countries have their own area within Usenet ("aus" is short for Australia), as do states ("oh" equals Ohio), and even some cities ("hsv" means Huntsville, Alabama.) It is beyond the scope of this book to list of all of them, and new groups spring up almost every day. Your access provider should have a list of newsgroups available, or you can look for a list on the Usenet newsgroup called news.announce.newgroups.

• • •

To make it easier to understand the ways these groups work, let me focus briefly on a newsgroup called misc.kids. I have a six-year-old daughter. Unlike Cheetah the cat, a daughter is not so easy to give away, so my wife and I have agreed to raise Maria to the best of our abilities. Some days, the best of *my* ability leaves me collapsed on the floor, near the point of weeping, while Maria promises to go to bed when and only when I give her one more cup of pudding and read two more Madeline books. At that point I usually dump the beautiful insomniac into my wife's lap and go to the computer.

The group misc.kids is not for kids, you see; it is for parents, and misc.kids is among the more highly trafficked groups on the Usenet system, with hundreds of fresh messages posted every day. Topics on misc.kids range from parental crowing ("I Have a Great Kid!") to serious tales of fear and woe ("Kid Won't Eat Anything but Macaroni, I'm Stumped!"). There are ongoing discussions about the advisability of amniocentesis, circumcision, and breastfeeding, and lots of talk about ways of exerting parental discipline, about the awful things older kids do to their younger siblings, and even about head lice. If you ever want a few chuckles, find misc.kids and read the messages concerning potty training. Turns out that potty training is hilarious (when it involves other people's kids).

What happens on misc.kids is just exactly what happens on each of the ten thousand or so other newsgroups—all that differs is the topic. For instance, late one Tuesday evening a woman named Zenia posted a message. (She wrote it on her home computer, sent it to the host computer of her access provider, and it showed up in misc.kids soon thereafter, where everyone could read it.) Zenia's message, appearing under the title "Am I Alone?," explained that she had two young children, worked a full-time job, dropped her husband off at work, picked him up, did all the housework and childcare, and even mowed the lawn. It was a swell life, except she could find no time to sleep. She asked for suggestions as to how to cope with this.

Nancy from Oak Ridge, Tennessee, was the first to respond.

"You're definitely not alone," Nancy wrote. "I have 3 kids, ages 9, 7, and 5. I get up at 3:30 A.M. so that I can get to work early and therefore leave around the time that my kids are getting out of school, eliminating the need for after-school care. My husband is on 2nd shift, which works out great in that he can get the kids ready for school in the morning and take them to school. The only drawback is that he and I never see each other during the week . . . of course, we have been married for 16 years, so maybe we're onto something here."

Other misc.kids regulars followed almost immediately with messages of the "hang in there Zenia" and "no, you're not alone" variety, and then a North Carolinian named Ed waded in with this timely question:

"Is your husband handicapped physically? If not, then why the heck isn't he doing some of the chores?"

Ed went on to explain how he and his wife Annette divide the work in their home—Ed cooks, washes baby bottles, does the yardwork, picks up around the house, handles the house-cleaning. Annette scrubs the diapers, cooks a lot of the dinners, does the laundry.

Susan Miller posted next, responding to Ed's message with this:

"Ed, you have given me hope. Do you have any single brothers?"

Others quickly chimed in with their own advice (get a maid, get a new husband, ignore the dirt). Then Kathy Leggitt wrote, "Well, after reading several responses on this thread, I called an errand service last night and hired someone to empty, clean, and refill my kitchen cabinets and upstairs closets. If I like what she does, she will get to do my laundry room after I get another paycheck. If it works out well, I intend to find someone to make and deliver meals too. Let my husband work on cars every night— I'm tired of it!"

A few cheers went up for Kathy, a few more people (men mostly) suggested that Zenia shop for a new husband, and then the whole issue seemed to die out. The last time I checked, there was one last posting on the topic. Gail Mellor of Kentucky wrote, "Keep in touch with us, Zenia. Let us know what happens. Do not give in to this. If it comes hard to think about yourself, think of what you are teaching your children about marriage. The best way to teach them that it is a partnership is to make it true."

Misc.kids is often filled with support and good wishes of this sort. The group, large as it is, seems to be sane, rational, and somehow not so electronically isolated. In Colorado, for instance, people who read and post to misc.kids have come together for summer picnics. Other people swap pictures of their children by mail. Some regular misc.kids users keep computer files full of useful information on key parenting topics, from discipline to disease, and they will send this info to anyone who asks. Maybe misc.kids is this way because almost everyone who posts is old enough to have had kids, or maybe they are just too worn down to be quarrelsome (unless you mention spanking).

Rec.gardens is another group where people help people. In fact, this group helped me through a horrible Pennsylvania winter. While my neighborhood had temperatures of twenty below zero and ten feet of snow on the ground, people from Florida were posting messages with titles like "Great News! My Roses Are Blooming." Screaming at these people to keep their damned cheerfulness to themselves was very therapeutic.

A list of recent subtopics on rec.gardens looked like this:

```
 1. Any Plumeria growers out there?
 2. Are spiders OK on cucumbers?
 3. Brown Turkey Fig leaves dropping
 4. Dead cucumbers—I give up
 5. Fusarium wilt on cukes?
 6. Groundhogs!
 7. Help! Duckweed!!
 8. Help! My Willow is sick!
 9. Mice in worm bin . . . now what?
10. Need SQUIRREL HELP
11. Overabundance of Rabbits
12. Potato Disaster . . . Mice!!
13. Squirrels Eating Tomatoes
14. Snails from Hell
```

You see now why gardening is considered to be relaxing? But even Thoreau had woodchucks in his bean field, and he could probably have used a group like this. For each of the pest- and blight-ridden subtopics above (Usenet people call such subject headings "threads"), there was the original question or announcement, then someone's response, then perhaps someone else's response that differed slightly, maybe a disagreement, then a clarification, some more helpful advice, and often the suggestion of a good book for more information.

This all takes place over time, of course. The first question might be posted on a Tuesday, and the answers posted over the course of the next two weeks, until interest in the thread dies out and the messages are deleted to make room for new ones.

The people on rec.gardens helped me keep the aphids from my roses, taught me when to harvest my crop of new potatoes, explained which kind of fencing would keep *my* groundhogs at bay, and assisted with the cantaloupe elevation project that I mentioned earlier. The rec.gardens group has good information (usually) offered in a friendly manner (almost always); it's fast, free, and you don't need to drive to the farmer's co-op.

But just as it would be dishonest not to mention the serious, useful groups, it would be a misrepresentation to ignore the frivolous and weird. Such groups—and there are plenty on Usenet—provide information no one can use, much of it offered rudely and contentiously. People drop in, do their damage, and leave with no accountability, and most discussion degenerates quickly into either obscenity, misinformation, or an outright attack on the person who first asked the question.

Many of the more bizarre groups can be found hovering in the "alt" category, meaning "*alternative*." One of my favorites is alt.destroy.the.earth.

The very name of the group, alt.destroy.the.earth, is wonderfully straightforward and unapologetic. These people are not content to just ruin the Earth's atmosphere to the point where human life can no longer exist. They want to vaporize the globe, destroy all traces of the planet, leave no outside chance that a single cockroach might survive and evolve all the way back up to hosting *Wheel of Fortune*. I assume they are kidding. They must be kidding. I hope they are kidding.

Conversational threads on alt.destroy.the.earth have discussed the feasibility of building thousands of space shuttles, hooking them to ropes, and hauling the planet off toward Mars, until the gravitational imbalance sends the various celestial orbs scurrying like billiard balls. There are a few bona fide astrophysicists in this group, and they purport to be working out the calculations. (Just good fun, right guys? Just kidding?) Another popular idea is to propel all the Earth's old tires, Goodyear *and* Firestone, toward the sun, until this added fuel raises the sun's temperature, evaporating the globe in one big cosmic meltdown. Call it accelerated global warming—just a little help from the boys and girls at a.d.t.e. There are plenty of nuclear options, of course, instances where we would all perish in some horrible conflagration—one fellow suggested condensing plutonium into powder and distributing spray bottles to every citizen.

And Clay Jones (so active on the Net, he has two nicknames, Space Ghost and Super Genius) posed this question:

```
Why do we want to make it a quick death? I
myself prefer the way we are already hurtling
into oblivion. When my city is under ozone
alert, I drive and fill up my tank. I'm the one
with the bumper sticker that says SPOTTED OWL
TASTES LIKE RIDLEY'S SEA TURTLE. I'm the one that
says "Kill a tree for Mommy." I triple- and
quadruple-bag things at the store where I work,
with paper bags, just to ensure we have to kill
more trees. Am I on the right wavelength here?
Many environmentalist whackos call me a fas-
cist. I prefer to watch them scream in agony
over a prolonged death while I sit fat and
sassy over a charcoal-grilled steak dripping
with fat, a beer in one hand and a smoke in the
other, with my lawn mower idling in the corner
of my yard belching out black smoke.
```

Pleasant, no? But when you come right down to it, his rant is funny (on purpose, I assume), and alt.destroy.the.earth has yet to destroy anything but the efficiency of my mornings.

A cheerier though equally baffling newsgroup of my acquaintance is alt.hi.are.you.cute. Not much problem with intellectual snobbery on this subject group. The purpose, as best I can discern, is for people to tell one another whether they are cute or not. Of course, participants in this group are talking by computer, so it is easy enough to lie. Nor does it seem to matter. Just say that you are cute, and you will be welcomed with open (electronic) arms.

Perhaps the reason I am so fond of this group is that the evening I discovered it someone sent a message from an address that ended with "house.gov." What this means in Internet idiom is that the individual on the other end was posting from a government account, specifically one connected to the House of Representatives. The important federal message asked, "Are there any cute girls out there?"

I was hoping to catch my local congressman cheating on his wife, or maybe even Newt Gingrich trolling for babes, so I quickly sent the house.gov person an electronic mail reply, asking, "Why is a House staffer (or are you a representative) posting to alt.hi.are.you.cute? Sounds fishy. Fess up or I will tell Bob Dole."

This apparently spooked the poor guy because I got a lengthy message back thirty minutes later explaining House policy on Internet use and making very clear that any and all alt.hi.are. you.cute activity happened very late at night, after business hours. For all the fellow knew, I might have been Bob Woodward at *The Washington Post.* I could feel the fear coming off the screen.

"I realize that America thinks Congress wastes their money," he wrote, "but let me assure you that I am in no way abusing the privilege of serving you." He admitted to being a legislative analyst for the Republican leadership and eventually asked me, "How cute do you consider yourself?"

Cute enough to know when my tax dollars are being wasted. That cute, at the very least.

People who spend a lot of time on Usenet are quick to point out what they see as a key distinguishing feature: no one is in charge.

While that claim is not entirely true, trying to explain why aptly illustrates one of the singular characteristics of the electronic culture. On Usenet, and across the vast electronic Net, lots and lots of people are actually in charge, to varying degrees, at various times, with varying results. So many different people are in charge of so many tiny electronic intersections, in fact, that it can become quite confusing.

At Penn State, for instance, the folks who maintain the large host computer that makes my Internet access possible determine which of the ten thousand newsgroups I can see. They make sure that groups dealing with sexuality, for instance, are unavailable to most Penn State users. Many other colleges and universities do the same. But if I really want to see these groups, I can get a second account through one of the commercial providers. (In fact, I did.)

The folks who run large host computers are called system administrators, and they also, to a certain extent, regulate which Usenet newsgroups get formed and which do not. But clever computer users are always finding ways around this. That is why we have a number of inane groups like alt.sex.fetish.startrek and alt.cows.moo.moo.moo.

"You can say anything you want," people will tell you, and again this is substantially true. Should I ever become obnoxious in my messages to other people or break the law, somehow bringing shame or strife down upon the Penn State system, they could shut me off in about three seconds in the same way Visa cancels a credit card: by invalidating my electronic-mail address and yanking my access. This would be true, as well, if I had an account with a big company such as Prodigy that discourages obscenity, or even with some small local service. But actual cases where people are tossed off are very rare, and if Penn State or any other host did throw me off the Net, I would only be off until I paid another access provider to let me on. There are literally thousands of ways in.

Lots of these system administrators are in charge of many different corners of the Net, but no one person, committee, organization, or government agency is in charge of the whole kit and caboodle. Standards differ from country to country, from account provider to account provider. There are so many people on the Net, coming from so many different directions, that no one really keeps track or can effectively censor what goes out. If you offer an unpopular or impolite opinion in a letter to your local newspaper, they can refuse to print it. If you do the same on a radio talk show, they can refuse to air your call or can cut you off in mid-sentence. But on Usenet, you pretty much determine for yourself what is acceptable and what is not.

Sometimes it seems like chaos.

Sometimes it is.

And Usenet keeps changing. It is getting more crowded by the hour, growing like electronic kudzu.

"Already," points out Steve Franklin, a physicist at Dalhousie University in Halifax, Nova Scotia, and a longtime Usenet user, the Net "has lost its personal feel," it is no longer an in-group of informed users from education, research, and industry. "Now, there are two distinct groups: those who know, and those who don't. There may be some bad vibes because the new users are looking for quick and easy answers to everything, and the knowledgeable users know how much work it takes to become accustomed to the Net environment. I welcome this expansion personally, but it will inevitably change the 'feel' of the Net."

Why so much growth, so much change, so many newcomers, so many people in such an awfully big hurry to enter these digital woods and look around for themselves?

One reason is certainly that it's "cool" to be on the Net. You could find discussions similar to those on Usenet elsewhere, by joining an organized group of hobbyists or enthusiasts, or by sitting in a coffee shop with your friends, but having it come across the phone lines and appear on your computer is simply more novel, more exciting.

Most people I know appreciate a good conversation, even an argument, and this technology offers us that. But perhaps more significantly, it offers us a convenient way to find talkative people and the chance to converse and argue with them *in the safety of our homes*, with near total control. Maybe that security is the allure, in a day and age when the man next door is as likely to pull out an automatic weapon as he is to come at you with a clever rebuttal. We can join the fray when and only when we choose to join it, we can do it from miles away, and we can shut it off whenever we want.

And the amount of information is truly dizzying. This is the Information Age, after all, and there is so much information out there on Usenet that you can dig forever and never reach the bottom of the pile. For some people, this presents a challenge, for others, something more like an addiction. I have heard countless stories of people who go searching on Usenet for just a few moments, to check one thing, and reemerge hours later, pale and jittery, totally oblivious to the concepts of time or hygiene.

I have been lost for hours myself in fact, wandering the highways, byways, and multiple dead ends. Around every corner, at the end of every keystroke, is something else, something that probably won't be that important, but it *might* be, so I keep going, keep checking the newsgroups, keep sending messages to the world, in case the next message is the one message I would regret having missed.

There are days when the Usenet seems nothing more than a waste of electricity: tales told by idiots, full of sound and fury, signifying nothing. But then I get a rapid answer to a nagging gardening question or read a message from some college kid asking for advice about a suicidal girlfriend, and I find myself hooked.

We are information junkies, after all, and Usenet is a strong dose of the purest stuff.

chapter three

PUBLIC RELATIONSHIPS

The Instant Appeal of Electronic Mail

Once upon a time, Katie Zitterbart met a dashing young musician named George. She was a freshman at Carnegie Mellon University. He was a sophomore.

The year was 1987, and Katie and George soon found that they had a good deal in common: they were bright, they loved music, they had mutual friends, and George's brother had even married Katie's cousin. In Katie's own words, she and George "did that fall-madly-in-love thing."

Some sixteen months later though, for all the usual reasons, the relationship came to a screeching halt. Heck, they were only kids. George moved to San Francisco. Katie moved on.

But the story took an additional turn in 1994, the year I first met Katie. Though she hadn't dated George for six long years, and hadn't even laid eyes on her old boyfriend for four, Katie was on the verge of moving three thousand miles away—to San Francisco, a cold, foggy, unfamiliar place—just to see if her relationship with him might be worth reviving.

And this was due, Katie told me, almost entirely to electronic mail.

Like Usenet, electronic mail is one of the Net's key attractions. No need to lick stamps. No need even to buy stamps. With electronic mail, you can send messages to Wisconsin or Italy as easily as you can send them across the hall, and, depending on traffic, your message will usually get there in a matter of seconds. Moreover, if you are on the right system, a note will flash on your computer screen telling you "mail delivered to goofy@disney.com" (or whomever). You would have to pay the U.S. Postal Service $2.52 for certified mail to get similar confirmation, and it would take days.

Katie Zitterbart is twenty-five, fair-skinned, with short-cropped red hair, a nervous laugh, and a master's degree in Literary and Cultural Theory. We meet at a sidewalk table outside Arabica, a coffee bar on Forbes Avenue in Squirrel Hill, the upscale section of Pittsburgh where Katie was born and raised. She tells me that her first experience with what the technical types call computer-mediated communication came while she was in college.

"Nobody talks at Carnegie Mellon," Katie explains, "they send E-mail. A lot of the population at Carnegie Mellon are very, very bright, but not necessarily socially skilled, and it helps a lot of them. Electronic mail is good for people who have a hard time dealing with other people."

For years, Katie used her E-mail access to communicate with

friends, with other students, and with her professors, but it was no big deal. She didn't become a geek or anything.

As for Katie and George, after their first mad love had dissipated into "just friends," she still heard news of him, through mutual acquaintances, but she was truly startled one day in October 1993 when an unexpected message popped up in her electronic mailbox. (The mailbox is sometimes called a queue—because when you get electronic mail, it sits and waits, sort of like waiting in line. When you turn on your computer and connect with your access provider, you will be alerted as to whether you have messages waiting. Punch a button or two, and you can read them.)

The unexpected message was from George. A friend had given him Katie's E-mail address, and George used this information to send Katie an electronic message, which, to the best of Katie's recollection, said, "I'm here, and I'm here because you're here."

At the coffee bar, I ask Katie, "How did this make you feel?"

She smiles sweetly. "He got on the Internet to talk to me, and I really thought that was very nice."

Some guys send flowers, but George sent electrons.

Katie E-mailed George back.

He answered.

She answered his answer.

It is very easy to answer electronic mail—depending on the software, it is usually as effortless as hitting one button ("respond"), typing a message of as many or as few words as you wish, and then hitting another button ("send").

"We started corresponding back and forth," Katie tells me. "You know, what's going on at work, what's going on at school —I hate school, I hate work. He's a musician, so he tells me about the band, about tours they go on."

Katie explains that George plays bass in a Bay Area band that is very, very hard rock. "Like Blue Oyster Cult." His ethnic background is half Scotch-Irish, half Japanese, and she says he is "a very interesting-looking man." And more than that, "He's a healer. He's on this earth to give people love. Everybody loves George."

She seems to struggle for a way to convince me of this, since George and I have never met. "He's the only guy I ever dated that my brother really liked," she finally says, "which is saying a lot."

Her brother is her twin, so I suppose it is.

The electronic correspondence between George and Katie went on for weeks before the relationship once again began to tread on serious ground. "One day he sent E-mail saying 'I'm really missing you, this is the closest we've been for years. Maybe I'm not over you. What am I going to do about my girlfriend?' And I was like, 'Nothing! I'm in Pittsburgh, you're in San Francisco!' But then I started thinking, did I ever quite get over him?"

Katie and George have given me permission to reprint some of the messages that once flashed their way across the complicated web of computer networks that connected these two old friends. Katie went through the messages first, however, and changed every proper name to an *X*, because there are other people involved.

The message below came early on from George, in reference to some problems Katie said she was having with another man.

I wanted to think this through as **objec-
tively** as possible. Before I start; DAMN I
MISS YOU KATIE!!! reading this letter was as
close as we've been for years. I'll *gladly*
:-) meet your man (if you and he want to)
because I certainly have more guts than this
hussie he hangs out with. OOPS I guess that
wasn't very objective! . . . as far as YOU are
concerned, I think you know yourself better
than I do. However, I'm intrigued by your sometimes slightly flippant reaction to the possible
end of this relationship, the oh wells and
such. Baby, where are YOUR feelings in all of
this? Are you being honest with yourself about
what you want in this relationship/life? (I'm
sure your generation-x angst makes this tough)
Two months is a good bit of time to think about
this one though. . . . Good luck, and I truly
hope things work out for the best. Take good
care of yourself. If you need me, you know
where to find me.

                                    -G

P.S. That you love somebody other than me
doesn't hurt me in the least. I am terribly
happy that you are in love and that you have
someone who loves you. Your happiness, regard-
less of the situation, is what I wish for you.

```
and to this end, I'll do anything I can to
help. I love you Katie Zitterbart. You deserve
the best. Rock on.
```

The asterisks and capitalization, by the way, occur quite often in electronic correspondence. It is not possible to underline, so these methods are used to indicate emphasis.

A few lines into George's message there is a little sideways smiling face :-) which is known as a "smiley" or, sometimes, an "emoticon." It attempts to substitute for what might be conveyed by facial expressions and vocal inflection in a real conversation. You can also wink ;-) look sad :-(or scowl :-{.

The next message comes a bit later. After Katie dumped the boyfriend in question, George sent this:

```
hi Katie! Have you found a new love yet? I hope
not. Will you wait for me? :-) take care, i
miss you much.

                          -G
```

George's digital sweet-talking worked its strange magic on Katie, and it was only a short time later that she decided to explore the idea of moving to San Francisco. So she wrote:

```
i am too much of a chicken to say this to you
even over the phone, and i figure that you can
blow off this message if you want to, and we
will never have to bring it up. here goes . . .

you were right about me lying to you about how
i felt when you came back for buggy, and you
were right about me lying to you about how i
felt about you after a couple of years.
```

if you accused me of lying to you about my
feelings for you now - you would be right as
well.

i think i am still in love with you, and don't
say "you always love the ones you love" or
something stupid like that. i freaked out when
i heard that you were planning to marry X, and
if that's what you want, then that is what i
want for you, but i thought you would like to
know what's up.

also, i am going to do my damndest to get out
there in the fall.

whatever it takes.

don't worry about me closing in on you if you
are still in a relationship with X, and don't
think that i have some stupid idea that we will
get back together and live happily ever after.
i mean, this may be some fantasy i have because
of cyberspace [what would old sigmund say, i
wonder?].

talk to you soon [i hope]. please don't hate me
for saying this in the first place and especially for doing it over the internet.

                              katie

Katie and many others on the Net don't capitalize the first letters of sentences, which makes the typing simpler. The reference
to coming "back for buggy" refers to a strange ritual at Carnegie
Mellon. Every year, the engineering students build go-karts and

recruit very thin, very small young women to pilot them in competitive races. The school doesn't have much of a football team, so this serves as a sort of Homecoming event for many at CMU, including Katie's friends. For those readers not familiar with CMU, understand that students at the Pittsburgh school are generally very smart—and often geekish as all get-out.

In any case, George replied:

```
Once, a long time ago, I was at a Primus show.
The fans were screaming "You suck!" which was
expected at Primus shows at that time. Les
Claypool (my personal god) walked up to the
microphone and said, "Tell us something we
don't already know."

In almost 5 years, nothing has changed.

Except everything.

                                          -G
```

At this point, Katie explains to me later, George asked her to quit sending E-mail for a while, because he was getting all nervous and confused. He wanted things to slow down.

Isn't that just like a man? You don't know what you got until it's gone, then you go off and get it again, and then as soon as you think you've got it, you're not so sure you truly want it anymore. These are hormonal problems all men face, however, and I'm not judging George. I have an old girlfriend, too, but as far as I know, she doesn't have E-mail.

As best I can decipher the exchanges above (it has been quite a few years since I was young enough to really understand),

George and Katie are both seeing other people (*X* and *X*) and neither one is particularly committed to the other person, though there is some reference to George marrying the *X* in his life. Then there is the Generation *X* angst that keeps them both from knowing what they want in a relationship. And then George goes to a Primus concert and the lead singer says, "Tell us something we don't already know." In this manner, love is found.

Man, oh man, I must be getting old.

Katie and George are not alone, by any measure. Stories of love and relationships have become so common on the Internet that they are rapidly becoming old hat. The Net world is turning into the singles bar of the nineties, and for good reason: the risk of sexually transmitted disease is wonderfully low.

I traded E-mail with Marcia, for instance, a California woman who met her fiance while playing a computer game on the Net—a game that involves a lot of role-playing.

"We initially met on TinyTIM," Marcia explained. "We didn't get to be on-line friends until we started talking more in depth on TrekMUSE, where we were hanging out while TIM was on hiatus."

In case your Internet Jargon Handbook has fallen behind the sofa, let me explain that TinyTIM and TrekMUSE are the names of particular role-playing games. Later on, when Marcia refers to "RL," she means Real Life, though understand that you should never, ever suggest to someone who plays such computer role-playing games that these games are not real life, or you will be called horrible names.

"When we met, we were both involved with someone else in real life," Marcia wrote. "I considered this a plus, since I was tired of having people with whom my characters on line got involved with expecting that that involvement was going to translate into RL."

But it did. After the RL relationships ended for both of them they met up in Colorado, where he lives. "When we met, we knew there was chemistry, and the rest reads like a classic long distance relationship."

Marcia cautions, though, that she and her fiance never really considered themselves a couple until they had actually met face-to-face. (Seems like a sound practice to me, but read on.) "I'd seen too many people claim they were going to marry someone they'd never met, then conspicuously avoid them after they'd finally met them in RL and found out that they weren't the person they thought they were: they were older/younger/fatter/thinner/taller/shorter/different ethnicity/inappropriate sex/richer/poorer than expected.

"The good thing about the Net is that it removes the dependence on physical looks for your impressions of people; the bad thing about the Net is that it removes the dependence on physical looks for your impressions of people."

I corresponded with other Net sweethearts, including a couple that met by E-mail and now have three bouncing kids, and a guy in Norway who wrote a poem and posted it to a Usenet group, traded E-mail with a woman in the United States who liked that poem very much, and eventually traded photos with her. They became engaged before they even met. Last he wrote, the wedding was set for July 1995 and he was saving his money for a plane ticket so that he could finally meet the bride-to-be.

There is a progression here, in case you didn't notice. Katie, of course, knew George, had once dated him in fact, though they had been out of touch for years. Marcia didn't know the man who would become her fiance at all, but she spent some time playing long-distance computer games with him before the relationship began to cook. The guy in Norway was just interested in poetry, and the love affair came on by surprise.

Many people, though, have begun to use the Net more intentionally. Like George, they are saying, "I'm here, and I'm here because you're here," but they are saying it to thousands of strangers, hoping the message will somehow wind its way through the immense network of networks and land in the electronic mailbox of their perfect but undiscovered mate.

On Usenet, for instance, statistics show that alt.personals is one of the most popular of the newsgroups, based on the number of people posting messages. I suspect there are hundreds more who just read it because it can be jolly fun. On any given day in August, you might find a list of subject headings such as these:

```
Any Kind-hearted Female in Toronto?
Beast ISO Beauty
BiF iso SM for copulatory activities
BiWM looking for MEN in NJ!
Cheesecake Wars: Philadelphia anyone?
Desperate humanoid seeks Spam-mate
FAT CHICKS! I WANT FAT CHICKS!
```

```
Hello from Boston
Hello from the Universe
Nice Guy in RI looking for a Nice Girl!
Pantyhose fanatic seeks Dom Woman
Seeking lady of Eroticism and Passion
Seeking warmhearted lady
Woodstock. I SURVIVED!!!!!!
```

There were 722 such postings to the newsgroup on the day I checked, all less than a week old. The contents ranged from very nice people wanting to meet other nice people for innocent companionship to offers that were not only immoral, and illegal in most states, but impolite as well.

The following messages were posted anonymously, meaning I have no idea who wrote them. (And of course, meaning no one really knows, except, we hope, the actual writer. They may have been written by men, they may have been written by women, they may have been written by your eleven-year-old nephew, so be careful when you respond.)

```
Subject: (None)
```

```
I wanted to post for my sister but she is
unaware that I'm doing this. But I'm sure if
someone nice responds, she may not mind too
much. It's worth a shot I guess. She is very
good looking but just not into the bar scene.
You're probably thinking how come she doesn't
have a husband yet, well I think because most
guys she dates are either jerks or don't want a
family and she does. Or single guys are intimi-
dated by her looks and maybe assume she's
```

already married. She is 5' 7", auburn hair,
hazel eyes, very thin, very good looking (Cher
look alike). She lives in South Jersey.

Subject: (None)

Hello,
We are a fun loving friendly couple, drug free,
non-smokers, no STDS, and only very very light
social drinkers. We are looking for a BiF to
join us for a fun vacation to Reno. We are
hoping to find someone we might be able to have
a real relationship with. We will pay for the
trip — you come along for the fun and adventure. You should be between 18 and 35, slender,
and attractive. And of course like threesomes.
We live in the Pacific Northwest. If you live in
Washington or Oregon it would be better, for
us. Hope to hear from you soon.

Subject: looking for zany S*F . . .

Somewhat crazy SWM would like to meet a similar
woman in the Minneapolis/St Paul area. Somewhat
crazy, you ask? Well, I would love to be involved in a plane crash - the ultimate roller
coaster ride! (If I survive of course . . .)
I try to avoid cracks in the sidewalk. I grin
insanely to myself all the time, mainly because
life seems so funny and futile. Worst of all, I
like Hillary Clinton. Gasp. I've been described
as being so intelligent that I'm stupid . . .

```
So if I sound like the wacky guy you've been
waiting your whole life to meet, here I am!!!
```

As with E-mail, responding to these messages is usually as simple as punching one button on your keyboard (the actual button differs, depending on your access provider and software), then writing your response. If you feel at all tempted to write back to any of the people in the sample postings above, though, call me first—I'll give you their electronic return address, and the emergency phone number of a competent psychiatrist.

Still, love is an odd and miraculous thing, and one never really knows where one might find it. To be honest, the examples above are a few of the more unusual and interesting messages, and yes, others are more traditional and sincere. The electronic personals, just like those boring old printed ones in your local newspaper, sometimes result in actual romance. In fact, the following message was also posted to alt.personals, and it was also anonymous:

```
Subject: ***THIS NEWSGROUP DOES WORK***

Hey all . . . Just wanted to drop a line to all
those out there in North America or the world
who are posting here. This really does work! I
was very fortunate to have hooked up with the
coolest person through a posting of my own. And
this person actually lives in my own city!
Imagine that . . . someone I can actually meet
instead of sending mail 800 miles away. Anyhow
. . . to all those who are frustrated because
of no response . . . keep on trying. You may be
pleasantly surprised!
```

• • •

Another interesting Usenet group is soc.singles, a place where conversation rather than proposition is the norm. You aren't even supposed to post personals to this group, though some people do. You are supposed to discuss issues of interest to single people, such as the following subject lines:

```
Being Single and Depressed
Height and Dating
E-Mail, Love, Sex and the Morning After
How to Pick Up Women
The Worst Pick-Up Line Ever
```

One striking difference on soc.singles is that most postings are followed up with a response, and then a response to that response, and then another, so that the conversational thread goes on and on. It is an interesting place to find out what men and women think, how they differ, and what particular issues will bring them to the edge of physical violence. (Answer: most.)

And every once in a while you get to watch as an angry misogynist shakes his on-line fist or some disgruntled female posts a message with a heading something like this:

```
ALL MEN ARE USELESS, DISGUSTING BRUTES!!
```

Of course, I can't really disagree. I would never date one.

There is an ongoing controversy in Net circles, by the way, as to why women are underrepresented—are they not as computer literate, or just less likely to fiddle away their time?—and whether they are made to feel welcome, or *too* welcome, on the Internet. Every couple of weeks or so a discussion bubbles up on one or another tabloid TV show about "Women Being Harassed on the Net" (check your local listings under *Geraldo*). The harassment in question is usually unsolicited E-mail. Some of it is just boorishness from horny young men, but some of it is the Net equivalent of an obscene phone call.

I went to my keyboard and distributed a question about this topic on various Usenet groups. In response, I received roughly as many messages saying that, yes, harassment does happen, as I did describing me as a dork-faced, pot-bellied pig with insufficient intelligence to pick my own nose. Some people clearly resented the question.

"I have been written to because I 'sounded cute' or because people thought I had a nice name," Cindi from the University of Kentucky wrote in response to my request. "One person actually asked if I was blonde because my name 'sounded' blonde. I've thought of having my i.d. changed to a gender-neutral name, but I figured it'd be too much trouble. The people who have written me have come from my own site and from as far away as East Asia."

A woman who goes by the ambiguous name of Dappy wrote, on the other hand, that she doesn't think gender really matters, "unless the person 'wants' it to matter. For example if I want to attract a lot of mail from men looking for sex, all I would have to do is act like I'm wanting sex. That is why I post in certain ways. When I do get the occasional mail asking me if I'd like to hot-chat via mail, I just very politely turn the person down." Dappy, she tells me, comes from a decoder her kids got in a Funmeal at Burger Chef.

But Shanen, a *male* who admits that his name is also somewhat ambiguous, doesn't talk sexy yet still gets harassing mail. He is a student at Penn State. "Guys on the Penn State system like to go down the Campus list and choose a woman at random to pick up," he wrote me. "Needless to say I have been selected at random many times. I actually counted them in the 93–94 school year and came up with 37." He says the experience has given him "a certain appreciation for what women go through—some of the lame lines and guys who just won't go away."

The fact is, almost every Internet site system administrator has had to deal with harassment complaints at one time or another. Katie, the Squirrel Hill woman about to move to San Francisco to see if her love might be rekindled, points out that this, however, is in no way unique to the Net.

"I get messages, but I just delete them," she tells me. "'Wow, you sound smart, are you pretty too?' or 'Do you have big breasts?' But just imagine being a woman going into a bar, it's the same thing. It's like a pat on the butt. I don't know why people complain about that sort of thing on the Internet, because you have so much control. There is absolutely no harm that can come to you."

As for George and Katie's love story, they did eventually agree that neither of them was entirely over the other, that it was worth another try, and Katie made plans to move to California.

"I'm not going out there just because he's there," she cautions, "because I think that would be a very bad thing, but he's definitely the reason why my choice was San Francisco. And wouldn't it just be the icing on the cake if this really did happen?"

She still hasn't seen George for many years, but she tells me that she knows him better than she ever has, and guesses that he knows her better as well, thanks to E-mail.

There is something—she struggles for the words—"more intimate" about sending E-mail than writing a regular letter, or even picking up the phone. "For some reason, I can say things more freely. I'm not a very good letter writer, but I'm a good E-mail writer. I think it's the editing. It's not as spontaneous [as talking directly], so you can choose your words more carefully. There have been messages that we've sent one another where we say, 'If this is really weird, just delete it and we won't bring it up again.' So you can say things in a way that is different than on paper or on the phone."

I don't know how far I agree with her on these last points. In my experience, E-mail is *less* intimate than a phone call or a good old handwritten note. There is no voice to convey meaning, and on E-mail everyone's handwriting looks the same. Most of the electronic mail I receive, in fact, even when it comes from good friends, seems chilly, too blunt, more like a memo than anything else. Perhaps the reason is this: when people write electronic mail, they know it will whisk itself across the Net in only seconds, and somehow this seems to encourage people to whisk their fingers across the keyboard almost as quickly. Brevity is certainly the soul of electronic communication, and I suspect old Thoreau, a man who disliked haste, would have disliked E-mail as well.

I wonder, though, if what Katie sees as intimacy might be the seeming *safety* of electronic communication. With E-mail, you never see the expression on the recipient's face, the reaction, and you don't hear the catch in his voice, so you avoid the risks you might encounter face to face or in a phone call. Or perhaps the sense of intimacy develops because E-mail can be sent so quickly, with a push of a button, and seconds later it arrives at its destination. This surely encourages the impulsive nature in the writer. *Am I sure I want to say that? Oh hell, just send it.* These are the voices in your head as your finger hovers over the send key. You write fast, you send fast, and sometimes your first impulse is more honest than your second.

As we finish our iced coffees, I ask Katie how serious she thinks her renewed relationship with George has become.

"As serious as you can be living three thousand miles away and not seeing one another for four years."

Will it work out?

"I don't know." She pauses. It is obvious that Katie is off-and-on embarrassed hearing herself talk about her old boyfriend George and their E-mail courtship. "This is weird," she says more than once. "This is not like me."

I ask Katie for her "best-case scenario," and she answers with a classic Freudian slip: "I land a job real fast in public relationships and live happily ever after with George."

A yellow truck double-parks across Forbes Avenue to unload cases of juice, and Katie stares thoughtfully into the distance through dark sunglasses. She has lived here, in this very neighborhood, almost her whole life. Her parents are here; her twin brother David lives nearby, as do more friends than she can probably count. Moving to San Francisco is no small thing, and she has obvious and understandable trepidation.

Will she miss everyone, I ask?

"My parents are buying a modem, getting on the Internet. The Internet is really going to be my lifeline to this city once I leave."

What if the relationship with George doesn't work out?

"I worry," she confesses, "that we'll be thrown together, declare our undying love, and then wake up one morning and realize that life has happened in the interim, and we have to deal with that first. And I don't want to get my hopes up, because I'm moving three thousand miles away and if I'm disappointed that would be enough to move three thousand miles back—and I don't want to do that."

Last I heard from Katie, she had left Pittsburgh for the West Coast. Her E-mail account at Carnegie Mellon was no longer valid, and she promised to let me know as soon as she found a new account. But it has already been a few months.

Love is an odd and miraculous thing, just like the Internet, and love can be found in the strangest of places, even on a wire, on an electronic lace doily spanning the globe. I like to think that maybe Katie has lost interest in the wire because she is happy now with George, and maybe they sold their computers and bought a futon. Who knows?

Katie does. She has my E-mail address.

If you are reading this, Katie, please write.

chapter four

MY BRAIN TURNS TO MUSH

The Strange Allure of Interactive Games

Falling in love over the Internet is one thing, but falling in love *with* the Internet is yet another. Tales of addiction and obsession, of people, almost always young men, who take digital bytes of information directly into their veins, who spend fifteen, eighteen, even twenty hours a day "logged on" to the Net, have been often reported by both zealots and skeptics, as proof of how wonderful this innovation can be, and as proof of its danger.

In my own quest to understand, my search for an answer to Thoreau's "of the devil or of God" question, I wanted very much to find such a person, sit with him, watch him compute, and then take the poor fellow to a sidewalk café, a *real* one, so that he could see what the rest of us look like, feel the wind in his hair. I wanted to find such a person, but I never imagined it would be so easy.

My introduction to Rob Dale came in the form of an electronic plea that he posted to the newsgroup alt.cyberspace:

```
Subject: I AM ADDICTED!! HELP!!

My name is Robert, and I am totally addicted
to "Cyberspace." I was first introduced to the
```

```
Internet by a friend. At the time I was only
MUSHing . . . I did that for the next seven
months. I spent the entire day, save breakfast,
lunch, and dinner, on the computer. Anything I
could do by modem, I would try. The semester
just ended at the end of April and I was going
to quit playing on the computer but, due to my
grades, I have to attend summer classes. Now,
I'm back to the same.
```

Rob is nineteen, tall, almost gangly, and clean shaven. On the day I meet him, he wears corduroy slacks, a Dockers shirt, and a Duke Blue Devils baseball cap, and seems altogether embarrassed. He wrote and posted the plea for help during the spring semester of 1994, but though I ask him more than once, he can't seem to tell me exactly why. He shrugs a lot.

Rob was born in Norway but moved to the United States, to Monroeville, Pennsylvania, when very young. Some of Rob's friends call him Roy, because he almost always wears corduroy slacks. When I ask which he prefers, Rob or Roy, he shrugs one more time and says, "Either."

Rob believes himself to be addicted to the interactive game of MUSH, short for Multi-User Shared Hallucination. Multi-user means more than one person can be playing the game at any given time. The Shared Hallucination part has to do with the nature of the game: the players create their own characters and their own rooms within the MUSH, fill the rooms with imaginary objects—both mundane and magical—and then interact with whoever comes to visit. It is all text-based, meaning words scroll by on your computer screen, not pictures.

"I just didn't know all you could do at the computer center," Rob explains to me. We are munching fries in the food court at a mall in Greensburg, Pennsylvania, a town about thirty miles east of Pittsburgh. I had offered to buy Rob lunch, anywhere he wanted, and he chose McDonald's. "I thought the computer center was just for word processing. I didn't know that much about the Internet. I knew it was there, and I knew you could do stuff on it, but I wasn't sure what."

His friend, a fellow student at the University of Pittsburgh's Greensburg campus, introduced him to the ins and outs of the Internet in one long day. After that, Rob spent "almost three days straight" on the computer, "except for breakfast, lunch, dinner, and about four hours sleep."

Rob, of course, was also taking classes at the time—Chemistry 2, which included a lab, a lecture, and a recitation; English; biology; and an introductory computer course—but he started missing more class periods than he made. "I wouldn't do anything all day, and then I'd go down to the computer center, a little while before dinner, mess around, and after dinner I'd probably go to the computer center until midnight and then, depending who was still up, go to their room, until about four or five in the morning."

His girlfriend, Kelley, was not pleased. "She hates computers. She doesn't understand why I do this."

His professors weren't too thrilled, either.

Before his obsession with the game of MUSH, Rob was an *A* and *B* student, but at the end of that spring semester, he came up with one *D* and three *F*s.

• • •

Visit the computer center on nearly any American college campus. Day after day you will see many of the same faces glued to the screens, bug-eyed sophomores, grinning until their lips hurt, unable somehow to pry themselves away. Walk up to one of them, say hello, and chances are he will act startled for a moment, then look right back at the screen.

Some of these young men and women are doing homework, but more of them are probably playing a MUSH, a MUD, or a MOO. A MUD is a Multi-User Dungeon. MUDs are more violent than MUSHes, because the object is often to kill or be killed. "MOO" stands for MUD/Object-Oriented, a distinction that is important to programmers and has nothing to do with dairy cows. Part of the appeal of these games is the way they let players interact—when I am playing the game and you are playing the game, we are playing with each other, not just with a machine. Many of the MUSH/MUD/MOOs are quite complex, and college students can't seem to leave them alone.

Why?

Let me advance three theories.

Theory One: They Are Addicted

The Internet is nothing more than an innovative electronic drug, and college students get this drug for free. (Of course, once they're hooked, they graduate, and then they get all jittery and nervous and have to pay corporate America for their next fix. Here is a fresh area of study for aging conspiracy theorists.)

This theory has the support of at least a few members of the mental health community. Dr. Michelle M. Weil, a California psychologist and authority on the effects of computer games, told the *Baltimore Sun* that games certainly can be addictive, and these on-line, interactive games are even more addictive than the games you buy in a box or cartridge. "With a (boxed) computer game," Dr. Weil explained, "you're always aware that it is a game." The fact that real people are on the other end of these interactive games, however, helps people lose track. They confuse the game with reality. "The underlying danger: the more time you spend facing the screen, the less time you spend doing other things."

Theory Two: They Are Learning Valuable Lessons

A second theory, hammered home by more than forty MUD users who responded to a few brief questions I posted on the Usenet group rec.games.mud.misc, is that the MUDs, MUSHes, and MOOs are useful, social, and educational.

A fellow calling himself TimberWolf, for instance, told me he was a student at USC in the school of architecture when he was introduced to the Internet. "I quickly found NetTrek [a Star Trek game, with graphics, where people take over planets and blow one another up] and MUDs and MUSHes. I spent a great deal of time on them, and at points decided to skip classes . . . This obviously had a lot to do with my lower grades . . . but I enjoyed the instant gratification and social interaction not available to me at the time. I turned to gaming for the fun and excitement I was lacking, and I still do."

Lavinia Hales, a recent Ohio State graduate, has spent up to fifty hours a week on a MUD. "What I like best about MUDs is the social atmosphere," she wrote me. "You can make friends and meet several people in different countries and regions of the U.S.

Some MUDFriends actually meet and they become real life friends. Many guys use MUDding as a nonviolent and healthy release of pent up aggressions. They can log on and kill things when they feel upset or angry over something."

Like their grades, maybe?

And Jessica Hekman, a student at Harvard who spends an average of ten hours a week on games, said she learned a new skill. "I like coding—in fact, I like writing MUSHcode so much that I took two semester of computer science this year in school."

Coding means programming—writing the commands (in computer language) that tell a machine what to do and when to do it. In a MUSH, for instance, advanced users can create an imaginary object (such as a robot bartender or a magic lamp) and write computer instructions that will allow that object to perform its designated function as other players encounter it, whether the creator is playing at that moment or not. It takes some work, some cleverness, lots of time, and lots of patience, and it can be a good way to learn.

Still, I have a third theory.

Theory Three: They Are College Students

College students, I have observed, love only one thing more than they love free beer, and that is to waste hours and hours of time, as much time as humanly possible, for at least four years. The Internet simply represents the newest and most efficient time-waster available, and college students are helpless in its grasp.

• • •

So that I can see a MUSH firsthand, Rob Dale takes me to McKenna Hall, the computer center at Pitt-Greensburg. McKenna Hall is the classic cost-efficient brick architecture you see on campus after campus. The Greensburg campus itself is a haphazard conglomeration of dorms and classroom buildings ringing a series of parking lots.

Before we can even enter the computer room, however, Rob has to check with the center's director and ask permission. He pops his head in the office door, chuckles nervously. "I have a guy here writing a book. Is it okay if I MUSH a little?"

The director looks up, looks me over, then laughs. "He brought you as an excuse, huh?"

I shrug.

Rob smiles sheepishly.

Rob has been banned from MUSHing because he and others were dominating the machines. "If they catch me," he had explained at lunch. "I'll get tossed out."

The director, though, nods his okay. "But just for today, Rob. Just for today."

This is not so uncommon. A large number of campuses have had to ban MUDs and MUSHes, or have banned them during certain hours. Others have a standing policy that anyone with a legitimate academic use, such as a term paper, can throw a MUD or MUSH user off any machine at any time. (On the other hand, students have found innumerable ways to fool computer center attendants. Rob changes the screen colors on his machine so that the student monitor can't see what he is doing from a distance. Moreover, the trend on many campuses now is to wire individual dorm rooms to the Internet, and machines in those areas can be used for anything at all.)

Rob sits down at one of the forty or so terminals in the room. It is about one in the afternoon. Only three of the terminals are occupied, but this is because Pitt-Greensburg is between semesters. Rob assures me that the blue chairs would be full if school were in session, and if it were later in the day. His classmates, or at least those most likely to explore cyberspace, most often roll out of bed around noon.

He plants his long fingers on the keyboard and begins to type. He types rapidly, scrolling from screen to screen, flicking the keys, barely stopping to read the text that appears. I finally ask him to stop. "What is it you're doing?" I ask.

"Oh, just showing you what's on here."

"But I can't see it."

He agrees to slow down, and I ask Rob if he could enter a MUSH and show me how it works. First, though, he checks his electronic mail but doesn't read more than one or two of the twenty or so messages waiting for him. He then spends nearly ten minutes sending electronic mail to himself to determine how long the mail takes to wend its way through the Pitt system and back into his account.

He eventually types the command "telnet" on the blue screen, followed by a seemingly random string of numbers. The numbers are actually the "address" of the MUSH Rob most often plays, TinyCWRU (CWRU stands for Case Western Reserve University, on whose mainframe computer the MUSH is housed).

The screen pops and blinks a few times, then the following words appear:

```
Welcome back to TinyCWRU! We are the world's
second oldest MU*, running TinyMUSH 2.0.10.p6,
the latest & greatest MUSH version.
```

This is followed by a short list of commands, and the information that six players are logged in. Rob checks to see who they are, and the following list appears:

```
Damien
puh
lynn
Juney
shadow of light
spyman
```

They are nicknames, obviously. Even Damien and lynn may be using pseudonyms, and as elsewhere on the Net, there is no real way of even knowing lynn's gender, or anyone else's. The nickname "puh" refers to Rob himself. He is reluctant to tell me what it means—he shrugs again, and says it is just a joke.

Juney, shadow of light, and spyman might be anyone, anywhere. Because these games are on the Net, a student like Rob at Pitt-Greensburg can be interacting more or less instantaneously with a MUSHer in New Jersey, another in California, and maybe a fourth person in New Zealand.

Nothing happens, then suddenly the computer screen displays this message:

```
You sense that lynn is looking for you in the
Pinnacle Revolving Restaurant, high atop the
Grand Hotel.
```

Lynn has apparently noticed (her computer tells her this) that puh has logged on, and she is attempting to make contact.

Rob types "visit lynn" and away we go.

```
The Pinnacle Revolving Restaurant, high atop
the Grand Hotel. This is the first floor . . .
There are four private tables here, numbered
1-4, and there is one main table. You are wel-
come to have a seat at any table you choose. As
the restaurant revolves, you can see various
panoramic views of the world of TinyCWRU out
the window.
```

Rob types "hi."

On the screen appears "lynn says hi."

Rob types "l lynn" (shorthand for "take a look at lynn").

On the screen, we read: "lynn has long soft brown hair, her skin is coffee with just the right touch of cream."

This may or may not be a true description of lynn, of course. What Rob is looking at is the text of the description lynn has typed in for herself. For instance, when we "look" at Damien, we learn the following:

```
Before you stands a dark and brooding figure
in a black suit. He is very tall and has jet
black hair. His eyes seem to be totally
black, but reflect light like a cat's. The
interior of his cape is bright red.
```

It is fantasy time here, time to become a vampire, a dashing prince, or a clever detective, but I cannot help but imagine that in real life Damien is actually five feet two inches, painfully thin, light-haired, blue-eyed, sixteen, and wearing baggy shorts in front of his dad's computer. We have entered the Shared Hallucination, and for a while Rob and I wander from the Revolving Restaurant to the Penthouse to the Study where Professor Mustard has the rope and the candlestick. Not much seems to happen. We just look around, say "hi" to any other players who happen to be in that room, check out people's descriptions of themselves, and meander along. Then Rob notices that a new player has logged on. The guy's MUSH name is CEE.

"Hey, I know him," Rob blurts out, rising in his chair. It is the most enthusiastic he has been all afternoon.

Rob sends a private message to CEE: "hey are you okay??"

Simultaneously, he explains to me that CEE is a friend, a fellow Greensburg student, now home in New Jersey. "He's a guy, but he's had cybersex with I think about five guys and about seven girls."

"Is he bisexual?" I ask naïvely.

"Oh no, he has a girlfriend."

"Why does he do it?" I ask, meaning, why would a heterosexual young man want to get on his computer and pretend to be female and have "sex" with other young men.

"He does it because it is so funny."

Rob types a message to CEE. "How many times have you had cybersex and with what?"

CEE answers "why?"

Rob: "For a guy writing a book."

CEE: "At least a dozen times and with both sexes."

Throughout this redundant, overlapping conversation between Rob, CEE, and myself, lynn keeps interrupting. Some of what Rob and CEE are saying is sent as a private conversation between them; some of it (out of sloppiness, I think) is sent in a way that makes it public to anyone on the MUSH, and lynn is understandably confused.

lynn: "huh? what does that mean?"

No one answers her, so she repeats the question. Then she repeats it again. Eventually, she tries a new tack. She is an inexperienced user, it turns out, and starts asking a series of beginner questions, of the "How do I do this? How do I do that?" variety. I can only sympathize.

Rob and CEE ignore her, trading howdy-do's and small talk with one another, until lynn finally types "I give up" and disappears from the MUSH.

It is not a game, in the classic sense. No one wins, no one loses, there is no score, and there is no point where the game ends. To the best of my observation, there is a great amount of wandering around, asking questions, being friendly, but there is no real goal.

If Rob's attention span is typical of his generation, our world is going to be in trouble in a few years. While simultaneously wandering the MUSH, trying to explain the finer points of the process to the writer sitting at his left elbow, and exchanging messages with CEE, lynn, and a few other Net travelers, he is also checking his E-mail accounts (he has more than one) and looking at messages in various Usenet groups. I am losing track rapidly and am not precisely sure to what extent Rob himself is able to make sense of the ceaseless input.

His fingers are constantly tapping. When there is nothing to type—for instance, while waiting as the computer answers his previous request—he strokes the outside edges of the keyboard or taps the table. His eyes are locked on the screen, and it occurs to me that Rob has barely made eye contact with me all day, even over our cheap lunch. He seems both eager to tell his story and embarrassed by it. Eventually he logs off the MUSH.

"So what do you like so much about MUSHing?" I ask, not having seen much to explain the appeal.

"You can do anything you want. It is not like society. There is no bias to anything. You can have any name you want. There are no arguments, no fighting. There is, like, no race. You can be yourself."

I point out the obvious. "You spend a lot of time on the computer, don't you?"

"I spend a lot more time on computers than with people," he admits.

"Are you more comfortable there?"

"I guess so."

"Why?"

"Around Greensburg, people are basically all the same, they're all here, everyone goes to the same mall, everyone does the same thing. On the Internet, you've got people from all over the world. Like, there are people on here from the Philippines."

It sounds good, and Rob is sincere, but I haven't seen him have any sort of substantive conversation with anyone all afternoon, and most everyone he has met on the Net has been a college student somewhere in the United States. I ask him what he talks to people about, people from the Philippines, or wherever.

"It seems most of the time I'm helping them," he answers. "I like helping people. You get to talk to them. It's kind of why I want to be a surgeon, too."

Rob had planned to become a cardiovascular surgeon, it turns out. At Pitt-Greensburg, he had been on the premedical track, though the low grades derailed that plan. A few weeks after we met, he E-mailed me the news that he had switched his major to Multimedia, the wedding of computers to pictures and sounds, which seems perfectly suited to his interests. Perhaps he will someday design a whole new breed of MUSH, one where we can see our dashing prince in bright color, instead of just watching strings of words that describe it all.

Eventually, Rob and I conclude our MUSH session and say goodbye. I gather my pen and pad, preparing to leave him behind in the computer lab.

"How was that for you?" he asks.

"Good," I answer. "It was helpful, I learned something. How about you?"

"Aw," he says, "it seemed boring."

So what is the appeal? If it is so boring, why do so many people play?

There are a lot of college students, sure, but others play as well: people much older than Rob, people with limited free time, programmers with expert skills, people who should know better. Why do they do it?

Rob sure seemed to be wasting an awful lot of time during the afternoon I spent in his company, but maybe having "the writer guy" hovering over his shoulder just made him too nervous. I have MUSHed myself, subsequent to my meeting with Rob. I never got deep enough into these games to become addicted, but I did get a glimpse of what is enticing about a MUSH. It can be a real kick.

One reason is that people act with striking benevolence in these role-playing games. There is certainly much more chivalry and gentleness on a MUSH than on the streets of your average American city, and who among us, especially when college-aged, hasn't yearned for such a utopia? The MUDs, the violent games, are just the reverse. We can kill, be killed, act out our aggressions with real ferocity, and no one gets hurt. No need to feel guilty. And we don't go to jail.

Intimate yet safe—we share our deepest fantasies, yet no one really knows who we are. The urge to fantasize is a very human urge, after all. What these interactive games allow us to do is share our fantasies (anonymously and safely), build on them, and act them out. Some of us take to the stage, but most of us are way too shy for that. Enter the Net.

It is no wonder that references to Star Trek and the role-playing game Dungeons & Dragons are so common in cyberspace—it is a world where one can, with ease, "boldly go where no man has gone before." There are plenty of other ways to fantasize, of course, but maybe the appeal of a MUSH is that having anonymous others read our fantasies, interact with our fantasy characters, and react to our fantasy actions makes it all seem more real.

   The computer is just so much plastic and silicon, but on the other end of the other computer, somewhere on a distant corner of the lace doily, there *is* another person, and for some of us, maybe that is just close enough.

chapter five

DIGITAL HUGS

The World's Biggest Support Group

OK, Tex, hold on!" Jim Shippey warns me by E-mail. "Supplemental Therapy is how I look at my use of the Internet. I currently maintain corresponding relationships with no fewer than six different women. Some are very casual, and some are very intimate. In general, the more intimate, the more helpful the experience. My therapist knows about my use of this medium, and he sees only positive results of the activity."

Jim is big, with big hands and a big handshake. He has dark curly hair and blue eyes, and seems confident, almost an extrovert. When I meet him outside the Floyd Heck Marvin Center at George Washington University, he greets me with a jovial "Hello, Professor." Jim is being polite, or, seeing as how I have pointed out more than once that nobody calls me Professor, stubborn.

The area of our nation's capital known as Foggy Bottom is between thunderstorms, so Jim grabs his bicycle helmet and we start looking for a dry place to talk. He doesn't seem nervous at all, considering the fact that I am about to interview him about matters that are highly personal and potentially embarrassing. But adult males with notebooks aren't what make Jim nervous. Women make him nervous, especially eligible women. He has, in his own words, always harbored "self-image, confidence" issues.

We settle down eventually at a group study table in the George Washington Library, and Jim, a twenty-eight-year-old returning undergraduate who was formerly a bookstore manager and security guard, fills me in. "When I first got here, George Washington University seemed a really daunting place. A lot of the students didn't seem very open and friendly. I felt like I really wasn't fitting in, so I took it upon myself to go and find counseling."

It wasn't what Jim found at the counseling center that eventually made life in Foggy Bottom tolerable, though. It was what he found at the computer center. Shortly after the semester began, Jim got a George Washington Information System student account. George Washington Information System shortens to GWIS, and the students like to call it Gee Whiz. Jim's account included a good measure of Internet access, and he soon found himself exploring Usenet groups like alt.horror, alt.cereal, rec.arts.movies, and some of the sex groups.

He would read the postings and giggle or shake his head. Sometimes he would send messages back to the newsgroup. At other times he would respond directly to the person behind the message, using electronic mail. Sometimes someone somewhere would send return mail, and soon enough he was trading E-mail with a host of people on a host of topics, and some of these people were of the gender that tends to make Jim stutter and sweat.

"I saw it as an opportunity to communicate with women, to find out about women's perspectives and views," he told me. "I started looking at it as something more than just playing around."

He told his therapist, who thought it sounded great, so Jim grew more diligent. For the summer, he found work at a Georgetown law firm, helping the lawyers sort out their filing system and trying to convince them to transfer their paper files to computer disks. After work almost every night, he would bicycle to campus, go to the Macintosh lab, and trade E-mail with women. Some nights he would spend three or four hours at this before putting his bike on the Metro and returning to his basement apartment across the Potomac.

A few of the women became regular correspondents, and he even told some of them about the problems that had driven him to seek therapy. He met a California woman on a horror discussion group, and they discussed books and movies, Stephen King stuff, until eventually the conversation grew more intimate. (Jim has asked me to call his California correspondent Judy, though that is not her real name.)

Before long, Jim and Judy were trading three or four messages a day. "I get off work, I come over here, I get on around seven, and depending on how busy she is, we trade mail for a couple of hours or so." Judy is at work during these hours, thanks to the time difference.

"What do you talk about?" I ask.

"We talk about differences between men and women."

"For instance?"

"Well, what's a reasonable idea of gauging, you know, what is the sexual appetite, what are the interests, because men in dating are so often expected to be the aggressor, and therefore the one who should know about this stuff."

There are moments during my meeting with Jim when I want to reach across the table and give him some friendly advice— *Listen, if you wait to figure out women before you date them, you will be waiting a very long time*—but I don't. He is getting professional help. I am just an amateur.

"That was something that I was kind of hoping we would get into in more depth," Jim continues, "but recently Judy has become a little reticent to speak about issues relating to sex, so I may not be finishing that line of discussion with her."

He seems troubled. His voice has a catch, and it would appear that all is not well in his electronic relationship with Judy. I ask him if this is true.

Jim nods. "We've been communicating so regularly that both of us have invested a lot of ourselves in it," he explains. "It has reached a point where she is feeling rather uncomfortable, mainly because she is—" He pauses here, seems unsure whether or not to finish the sentence, but eventually does "—she is married. She's married and she's forty-two years old, and I guess when you start finding that you are getting support somewhere else that maybe ideally should be coming out of your marriage, then I guess you start questioning the underpinnings of the marriage, and that could be kind of scary."

In my attempt to enter the electronic woods with an open mind, with Thoreau's sense of discovery, I found one of the biggest surprises to be the extent to which folks like Jim Shippey are turning to this cold, distant, faceless electronic medium for human support and understanding. Therapeutic uses of the Internet are not only common, they are busting out all over. Consider this selected list of some current Usenet newsgroups:

```
alt.abuse.recovery
alt.recovery.addiction.sexual
alt.recovery.codependency
alt.recovery.religion
alt.support.anxiety-panic
alt.support.asthma
alt.support.big-folks
alt.support.depression
alt.support.diet
alt.support.epilepsy
alt.support.loneliness
alt.support.stuttering
alt.support.tall
```

And this list is not even close to complete. A number of other medical problems, from cancer to ringing ears to irritable bowel syndrome, have their own Usenet discussion groups, as do smokers, nonsmokers, and men who feel they have been screwed over in divorce court. These are some of the liveliest newsgroups on the Usenet menu, and often the most fascinating.

Moreover, literally thousands of other such groups, including a host of regularly scheduled Twelve Step meetings, exist just outside the Internet, on local bulletin board systems and on most of the major on-line access providers. America Online, for instance, has Monday meetings for infertility, chronic fatigue, and "Marital Blisters." On Tuesday, there is an AA meeting, a support group for depression, one for eating disorders, a meeting of Adult Children of Alcoholics, and a forum for Panic Support. On Wednesday, there is a breastfeeding discussion, and groups for cerebral palsy sufferers, abuse survivors, and parents of gifted children. And finally, there are hundreds of electronic mailing lists dealing with these issues. (Mailing lists are similar to newsgroups, but instead of the messages being posted on a public bulletin board, those interested must subscribe, and subsequently all the public messages are E-mailed right to the subscriber's in-box.)

If anything whatsoever is bothering you (Marital Blisters?), it is probably bothering someone else as well, and if you want to talk with someone about this problem, the Internet is fast becoming the place to do it.

On the other hand, if you don't have problems (which is known as denial, and someone will be starting a group for that soon), or if you do have problems but don't really want to talk about them, there is the option of eavesdropping. Reading groups such as alt.support.help-I'm-miserable can become an addiction of its own.

People, you see, share the most intimate topics imaginable on the Internet. Every time I think I've seen it all, I log on and find something even more surprising. Sickness, death, love, sex—all of these are regular themes. On the Net, like on television, the people are real, the problems are urgent, and you can quickly find yourself involved.

One day I ran across a young man's poignant note about his suicidal girlfriend, his love for her, and his frustrated attempts to find her some form of help. "When she is well, she is the one for me, the one I've always wanted," he wrote. "But when she's depressed, I can't imagine living with this woman, at least not for all time. How can I stop from losing her?" The outpouring of sympathy and what seemed to be actual, useful advice was immediate and sincere. I sent the guy a note myself. Heck, it was easy, and I felt pretty bad for him.

Reading these postings can be a bit like reading "Dear Abby," only the advice is not censored, punches are seldom pulled, and there, hovering at your fingertips at all times, is a button on the keyboard that will let you jump in with your own two cents.

Try ignoring that button for more than a few days.

Go ahead, try it.

And finally, unlike "Dear Abby," but a lot like *Days of Our Lives*, you can follow these people's stories well beyond the initial request for advice. After the posters tell the whole world what is mostly none of our business, some of them disappear, but a good number come back a few weeks later to let us know how it all turned out. And then people respond again, they give fresh advice, they argue with one another, disagree on what should be done, they say "I told you so" over and over, until it hardly seems like the original poster's life is his own.

Just like a family.

Take a fellow named Steve, whose marriage fell apart in a particularly nasty (and lurid) way. He had been chronicling the downfall on soc.couples, and when the worst happened, he went to the Net with this posting, which I've quoted with Steve's permission, though a few key names have been changed.

From: Steve
Newsgroups: soc.couples
Subject: Caught Wife Cheating—the final straw
Date: Mon, 13 Jun 1994 08:04:52

This weekend really made the finality of my
relationship with Nicole sink in. Sally told me
her husband and my wife were at a campground
nine miles from my house. I called the campground office to verify this, went there, and
found their camp. Jim and Nicole left the front
door open enough that when I walked by I could
see them disrobed and entangled with each other.

I said something so Nicole knew I was there. I
left and later she came to the house and admitted she has been committing adultery nonstop
for several weeks. Her admission after all the
lying only made the lying and the adultery more
real in my mind. She said she wanted to be
friends after we got divorced and tried to hug
me. For the first time in my life I pushed a
woman away from me as I felt complete disgust
and revulsion of her and told her that I am not
even interested in remaining friends.

We discussed getting together to write up a
property settlement and she informed me she
plans to use her attorney after all.

I can hardly wait to get all of this behind me
and forget the past decade of knowing her. The
future has to be brighter!

                              Steve

Many, many people responded, of course, with all manner of advice, including the decidedly unromantic but practical Dennis, who said:

```
Steve, I would strongly suggest hiring your
own attorney, even if all he/she has to do is
review the proposed settlement. Nicole is no-
where near as emotionally damaged as you are,
and could use this very strong advantage
against you. Take it from someone who lost
*everything*, including my son.
```

Steve took the advice, it seems, because he posted the following philosophical message one day later:

```
From: Steve
Newsgroups: soc.couples
Subject: Re: Caught Wife Cheating—the final straw
Date: Tue, 14 Jun 1994 08:21:30

Hi,
Nicole and I both have our own attorneys now.
To make things simpler however, she came back
to the house last night and worked with me on
listing our joint and separate property and
dividing it up. We had no problem deciding how
to divide the property. We just have to settle
on what happens when we sell our house and
we're done.

What seemed different to me though last night
is that Nicole seems like a complete stranger
to me. She is not the woman I met ten years
ago. This entire affair has altered her per-
```

spective on life to one of being a flighty free
individual precisely at the point in my life
where I feel more settled down than ever.

It seems that maybe men and women grow in opposite directions. When I was younger, I did not
really like being settled and younger women
often focus heavily on settling down and raising a
family. It seems that by the time we are into
mid 30s and 40s that men get much more settled
down and women are more assertive and adventur-
ous in their lives.

When I was 20 years old, I really had a LOT of
confidence that I knew what life was all about
and that I could succeed. At 40 years old, I
don't know anymore. I don't have a clue what
life is all about, I feel lost. It seems to
me there is only one thing worth living
for—GIVING AS MUCH LOVE IN THIS WORLD AS
POSSIBLE.

And people responded to this one, too, of course. A fellow
(also named Steve) had this to say:

You are starting on the right path. Many of us
were concerned because you would not let go of
your first wife even though all of the signs
were there; however, you are learning and you
are human. You are not the first to live through
this and you won't be the last (unfortunately).
Good luck and give yourself a break.

Tim, though, was not quite so gentle. He wrote:

```
You sound like you could use a good dose of
counseling. There are books about divorce
recovery that are helpful . . . I'll have to
find a title and post it. You know, I may sound
a little unfeeling to say this, but "GIVING AS
MUCH LOVE IN THIS WORLD AS POSSIBLE" is not the
one thing worth living for. In fact, if your
only purpose in life is to "give love" you
sound a little . . . codependent or something?
```

Codependent? Internet exchanges like this could make each and every one of us codependent in roughly the time it takes to say "emotional enmeshment." Read enough on the various support groups and you'll have trouble sleeping nights. (Or you'll sleep better, with the warm feeling that your own problems seem awfully light by comparison.)

The thread "Caught Wife Cheating—the final straw" went on for well over a week until most every angle was seemingly exhausted, and then the soc.couples regulars moved on to other bits of domestic intrigue.

But, really, is this is just electronic exhibitionism, or does it actually work? Do the support groups support? Do people feel better, tackle their real or perceived problems, get well?

I posted my questions to a handful of the more popular support groups, and the response was rapid, vast (at least fifty people E-mailed me back in about two days), and overwhelmingly positive.

"When you are down and out," wrote Sam, a regular reader of alt.support.depression, "you don't want to go out, you don't want to meet others, you just want to be by yourself. The impersonalness of computers allows you to both reach out and hear others and be alone in a safe place."

Mary-Anne, posting from Massachusetts, wrote, "If I'm one fat woman posting in, say, ne.singles [New England singles], and someone decides to verbally abuse me on account of my weight, I am alone. If I'm one among many fat people posting in, say, alt.support.big-folks, then anyone who abuses me will get argued with. The fact that people with the same sympathy gather together make a group a safer place."

The notion of a safe place was a recurring theme—a newsgroup of this sort is electronically insulated, it is usually full of like-minded people, and like-minded people are more likely to agree with you than jump all over your case. This can be important when someone is hesitant about discussing a personal issue. Catherine from Philadelphia, for instance, pointed out the important support found in groups dealing with gay, lesbian, and bisexual concerns. (One of these is soc.motss, which means "members of the same sex" and has nothing to do with clever french sayings.)

"When I was first coming out to myself as a bisexual, I started reading the gay news group," Catherine wrote. "It was an absolute godsend. Without anyone being able to see me, I was able to listen in on a big discussion between all kinds of gay people. Some were very out and in your face, others were just coming to terms with the idea of being gay. It was an amazingly positive experience to be able to hear my 'peers' say that they had had feelings just like mine, and to hear them defend all of us from the homophobes."

My decidedly unscientific survey yielded unanimous agreement that the various support groups make people feel better, safer, less alone. But are they getting good advice? Can everyday people on the Net, most of them not trained professionals, really offer proper counsel?

I asked an expert, John M. Grohol, an on-line advocate for mental health issues, founder of many of the Usenet support groups, and comoderator of sci.psychology.research. "The first thing you learn in graduate school," he warned me, "is that professionals do not give out advice. When someone walks into a therapist's office, they've already heard all the advice—they don't want any more! Having said that, from all the advice I've seen posted, I believe most of it is well-intentioned, generally sound, and full of common sense."

But ultimately, I asked him, is what happens on these groups really useful? Or is it just a temporary fix, a chance for people to spill their guts on-line and feel better for a few days?

"People's own issues are their own and they aren't likely to be solved by a few messages on a support group," Grohol said. "It may, however, help them get started on feeling more comfortable talking about such things to their family, friends, and therapist. Support groups—even in the real world—aren't meant to replace therapy, but are meant as an adjunct to therapy."

He noted finally that, according to the most recent research, those who actually post to a newsgroup make up only a very small percentage of those who actually read the newsgroup, in the 3–5 percent range. "In other words, most people are 'using' the support newsgroups silently, without ever posting. They're getting their support through just reading other people's messages. This," Grohol explained, "is a common effect found in real support and therapy groups as well."

Jim Shippey, the George Washington University student who has trouble with the opposite gender, is going beyond just reading support groups, however—he is actively using the Net for therapeutic reasons, working through his "issues" in a deliberate manner.

"On the Net," he says to me, "it all has to go out from your words, and it's sort of an equalizer that way. You can actually talk to someone about a sensitive issue, without being too invasive."

He seems to prefer electronic mail to posting on the public newsgroups, and this probably makes good sense, since the problem he is tackling involves one-on-one shyness.

"I've saved a lot of posts from certain people with a certain romanticized idea that, you know, back in the last century there have been some great relationships of correspondence which took place with nothing but pen and paper. What you see now is that the same sort of thing occurs over electronic mail, but instead of the matter of years or decades, you're talking about months. You can exchange four or five times in a given evening perhaps. It's accelerated."

Jim sent me copies of some of the E-mail messages he has shared with Judy so that I could get the flavor of what was discussed. What struck me was how different his personality seemed when expressed with electrons. Jim spoke slowly, carefully, cautiously with me in person, but he was downright florid on the E-mail page.

Here, for instance, is part of an E-mail note Jim sent in May, when Judy was about to leave for a camping trip:

```
Date: Tue, 3 May 1994 15:41:32 -0400 (EDT)
From: James Shippey
To: Judy
Subject: Re: Long hugs
```

This will be the last of my electronic legacy until you get back. I have definitely developed a dependence on your kindness, insight, wisdom, intelligence, sensuality, objectivity, subjectivity, sensitivity, awareness, humor, experience, perspective, spark, imagination, warmth, intimacy, concern, caring, affection, praise, plaudits, and everything else which constitute the whole of you, Judy. How I will want to share my experience with you!

Now help me with this: I am a female *charmer*? I beg you to explain what you can see in me as far as that goes. I wish to be courteous and ingratiating with most women, and yet so few care for my manner. It seems to be the old saw about why nice guys finish last. I knew a guy, a fast crowd guy, who was an absolute monstrosity towards his girlfriends (although I never saw him get physically violent with them, as it probably would of ended with him and me getting violent [maybe he feared that!]), and invariably he was the heartbreaker. Why do women long for that? And back to me: isn't what I offer a more pleasing option?

As far as to where I learned my behavior, all
I can say is that it wasn't from my parents!
That's where I learned my capacity to hate
. . . . sorry to say. That's a by-
product of an ugly divorce.

And now I bid you bon voyage! I hope that you
get held more than you expect this week. The
outdoors can be rugged and challenging, but they
also can be very romantic. A wonderfully strong
hug and a kiss on the cheek to send you off, and
write *as soon as you get back*!!!!! We're going
to have to start comparing notes on THE STAND!

Have a Great Vacation, you fabulous woman, you!

-Jim

And when she got back:

Date: Thu, 12 May 1994 17:02:05 -0400 (EDT)
From: James Shippey
To: Judy
Subject: You have returned!

Happy, happy, joy joy! I'm so glad that you are
back! How was your trip? Was it great to get to
know your husband all over again or was it same
ol', same ol'? Did you give Jack London a run for
his money?

It would seem that Jim has his problem licked, the problem of
talking openly with the opposite sex, at least as long as he stays

in the Macintosh lab, but there is that other Big Question everyone must be asking by now:

Is this leading anywhere? Can Jim transfer his newly found Internet charm and grace to flesh-and-blood situations?

The jury on that one seems still to be out. Jim did have a blind date over the summer, but only one, and though his friend Judy gave him some good advice—the female, she told him, is probably even more anxious than the male—"Ultimately," Jim tells me, "it wasn't the greatest time of my life. We met, and we talked, and I'm glad. It was a good thing to do."

They just didn't hit it off, however.

I ask Jim if his letter-writing relationships were giving him any greater confidence around women, real women, the women he sees every day at work and in class, or if he was perhaps just retreating deeper into an electronic cocoon.

"In the short term, it has been a replacement," he answers. "In the longer run, I am gaining more information, and it has led to some socializing outside of the computer lab, and that has been good."

But the sentence trails off. He doesn't seem so sure of that answer, he doesn't seem to have much confidence in his own words. Will he try another blind date?

He laughs. "Sure, but how soon I can't say."

"You spend a lot of time on-line, don't you?"

"I do."

"Why?"

He smiles, shrugs his big shoulders. "It's fun, it's entertaining. It's cheap."

• • •

The Net is all those things, and again, I do not dispute that these digital relationships can be helpful. That is the positive side.

The negative?

Well, maybe there is a point where hiding behind the screen becomes a crutch. Trading E-mail is a sort of relationship, but it is not a full relationship—not even close. I worry about a day when we all communicate this way, choosing our words maybe *too* carefully, just as carefully choosing our natures and dispositions, our on-line names, and even our genders, based less on who we are than on what we wish to project.

I worry whether we will become something less than warts-and-all human beings and something more like fast-typing press agents, spin doctors for our own personae. What if electronic communication was all we had left, just words on a screen, cryptic electronic addresses that could just as easily be across the hall as across the world?

I like to imagine myself like the hero of some corny science fiction story, the guy who sneaks out of his high-rise one day against all regulations, ducking the video surveillance, dismantling the motion detectors, just to meet with a flesh-and-blood friend behind the nuclear power building, just to stand close to another human being for a moment, to breathe on someone, to feel that someone breathe back at me.

We are not all of us as pretty as Mel Gibson, maybe, but when I show my true face, I assume that means the underbite, the slightly crooked glasses, and that bit of my hair that always seems to stick up in back.

That's me, too.

Like it or not.

chapter six

HANGING OVER THE ELECTRONIC FENCE
Inside a Virtual Community

At first glance, they look like any other group of suburban friends gathered on a Sunday afternoon, half of them manhandling an innocent volleyball, the other half hovering over a platter of barbecued chicken and drinking homemade beer.

Yet they aren't a normal group of friends, they are what Net people call "virtual" friends, an electronic community. They are patrons of the Cellar, one of thousands of small bulletin board systems (BBSs) scattered around the world.

What makes the Cellar and other BBSs different from the Internet is mainly a question of size. While an estimated 30 million people use the Internet, about 150 people dwell in the Cellar. While Usenet has thousands of discussion groups available, the Cellar has just over twenty-five. Cellar owner-operator Tony Shepps, in fact, calls his diminutive BBS the Anti-Net.

"If the Net is the equivalent of an encyclopedia," he explains, "we're the equivalent of a dusty old novel. If the Internet is the world's biggest mall, we're the friendly coffee shop down the street."

In other words, the Internet is dizzying and wonderful, allowing us to trade our thoughts with Chileans, Finns, Germans, and over a million American college students, but at the end of the day, we haven't grown too intimate. On a small system like the Cellar, however, we exchange ideas day in and day out with a small pool of regular users, quickly finding and identifying those people who seem intelligent (they agree with us, or disagree in interesting ways) and those who seem to have left their brains in a small sack under the bed. Before long, we rely on the former group, testing theories, asking advice, following up trains of thought, sharing the occasional joke, until some of our best friends are nothing more than words on a screen.

Proponents of these virtual communities say that electronic relationships of this sort can be as real as relationships that take place off-line. In many cases, they say, electronic pen pals become more like neighbors than the people who actually live next door.

Well, that sounds good, doesn't it? But as part of my ongoing investigation into what people are really doing out there in our electronic culture, I really wanted to get a firsthand look. Are these electronic communities something new and wonderful, or are they just high-tech hidey-holes, so much sand into which the ostriches among us can stuff our heads?

Fortuitously for me, the Cellar has one other distinguishing feature—its people have feet. Every so often, maybe once or twice a year, they power down the 486 towers, flip off the high-resolution monitors, scrub their pale faces, and leave home. They call it a GTG, as in "get-together."

Even Thoreau left his cherished woods to go huckleberrying

once in a while, so when Cellar-owner Tony was nice enough to invite me to a barbecue in his backyard, and didn't even ask me to bring the hot dog rolls, I accepted his offer.

The Cellar is based in Montgomery County, Pennsylvania, about forty-five congested minutes north of Philadelphia. Tony lives in Collegeville, so known because of Ursinus College, though Tony's comfortable split-level home sits far from the center of town, in one of the mushrooming suburban developments eating up almost all of the region's former farmland.

When I arrive, Tony's house is packed with folks, around thirty of them, and his wife looks understandably nervous— more than a few unattended children are tearing up and down the stairs, looking for loose glassware. The adults are all white, seemingly middle-class, of varying ages, and few are obvious computer nerds. Judging from the volleyball action in the backyard, not many of them will be headed to the Olympics any time soon, but they are certainly nice enough to a visiting writer, and boy can they cook.

The menu includes chicken, salmon, catfish, cole slaw, potato salad, cut celery and carrots with fattening dips, various other munchies, and some of the best chocolate chip cookies I have ever scooped from a plastic plate. A few of those attending the GTG are old friends from other GTGs, while some know each other only by their computer addresses (so-and-so@cellar.org) and are busy placing faces with the names.

Adam Zion, at twenty-three one of the Cellar's youngest users, has a forceful, intense manner that suggests a future in politics; instead he is preparing to enter a postbaccalaureate premedical program at the University of Pennsylvania. "Most online communities are just that—on line," he tells me. "You ask, 'Let's meet,' and all of a sudden people stop talking. Here you say, 'Let's meet,' and people say, 'Where?' Big difference."

Adam and I are chatting in the basement of Tony's home, in a boxish room stuffed with furniture, bookshelves, milk crates, two computers, and six modems. The modems handle the incoming calls, which means only six users can call at any one time. This room is the Cellar's modest control center.

"I like being on-line with people who are genuinely mature," Adam continues. "I like being on-line with people who aren't going to flame you when you post something. They may argue with you, but I've never seen a genuine flame (a deliberately insulting message) on the Cellar. That is *unique*. Flaming is a real problem in the BBS and Internet world." He pauses, opens his hands, and indicates the people outside. "This is a community that happens to be virtual rather than physical. A lot of BBSs are just service providers. But this is a *community*."

I speak also with Bruce Morgen, a jolly fellow with long, graying ex-hippie hair, a wonderfully fuzzy beard, a big belly, and a yellow T-shirt that says "ALIENS BACK CLINTON." The T-shirt displays the cover from an old issue of the *Weekly World News*, a photo of the candidate enthusiastically shaking hands with an extraterrestrial. Bruce looks decidedly unconventional but admits to "two kids, a wife, the whole nine suburban yards."

"The Cellar is a very convenient community when you have a busy life," he tells me. "People with disabilities aren't the only ones who don't get out. People with young families have a tremendously hard time getting places. The Cellar is a way for me to have a relatively friendly and often interesting social life that I can basically handle in an hour or hour and a half a day."

Bruce has bounced around the Internet and logged on to numerous other BBSs, but he says the Cellar is different. "The Cellar is prescreened for intelligence. The stupid modemers [his term for people who use a modem] or immature modemers are basically on-line to get pirated software or game hints, and that's not what's on the Cellar, so they get bored and leave." He waves his arm, indicating the friends and strangers standing around the table with plates full of food. "The whole pulse of the Cellar seems to suit me. I find people I have a lot in common with, and intelligent people that I differ with quite a bit, and that's good."

The people I speak with seem pretty content with the small corner of the electronic world they have staked and claimed, and the Cellar's ratio of men to women seems more balanced than some areas of the greater Net. Bronwyn, a nurse, with dark curly hair, a bright smile, and two daughters, tells me she has been on the Cellar for two and a half years. "What I like is that it's open all hours," she jokes, "but you don't have to go anywhere or have anyone over. You don't have to clean the floor, you don't have to stock the fridge, you don't have to worry about a babysitter. You can access it at any time." She "lurked" for months, reading messages posted to the various subject boards but never replying, but now she is a full participant in the daily exchange of ideas. "People are perfectly willing to slap you across the face and say 'you're wrong, wrong, wrong, wrong, wrong, your logic is flawed, everything about this is faulty,'" she tells me, "but having said that, though, they are forced to back it up. 'Here's where your logic is flawed.' It can't just degenerate into insult, it goes into argument and debate. There is a delightful ability to bat something back and forth until all the meaning is wrung out of it."

What distinguishes these people, it seems, beyond their cooking and conspicuous lack of volleyball skills, is that they *do* love to argue, they are full of ideas, they love to talk, and they are excited about just how much arguing and talking they can get done in front of a computer. They are also excited about Dan and Suzy, and many insist I talk to *them* next. So I do, dragging Dan and Suzy down to the basement so we can hear one another speak.

Dan Reed and Suzy Freeman met on the Cellar, planned their first date on the Cellar, and are now engaged. (This is becoming common enough in the Net world, of course, so much so that some people find it mundane, but Dan and Suzy will be the Cellar's first marriage, and everyone seems proud.) They are both in their twenties; he is an automotive technician, she a database manager. They will make an excellent married couple, in my opinion—they already finish one another's sentences.

"By the time we dated, I knew a lot about him already," Suzy tells me. "I knew what he liked, what he didn't like, what his political beliefs were. The weirdest things about him, I knew already. It wasn't like I had any big surprises."

Dan concurs. He thinks trading messages on the Cellar is an excellent way to become acquainted. "There are just things you can find out about somebody that you really couldn't just if you'd gone out on a date."

"Our first date, we spent the entire day, from ten in the morning until eleven at night, together," Suzy points out, "and we were comfortable. Which is pretty rare . . ."

"Rare," Dan says, "on a first date."

The Cellar is hardly the only virtual community, of course. One of New York City's many is ECHO (East Coast Hang Out); in Austin, Texas, they gather at the Spring; there are many others.

The most famous is certainly the WELL, based in San Francisco. One of the reasons the WELL is so well known is that lots of interesting, innovative, computer-fluent, and drug-addled people live in the Bay Area. Another reason is that the founders of the WELL passed out free memberships to journalists and writers back in 1985, when the system was just starting up, and amazingly there were approximately 17 billion subsequent stories written about what a neat place it was.

Coincidence?

The WELL was the brainchild of Stewart Brand, publisher of *The Whole Earth Catalog*. WELL stands for Whole Earth 'Lectronic Link. The first director-operator was Matthew McClure, a veteran of the 1960s commune movement, and there is certainly a communal atmosphere to this and other virtual communities—an inclination to let the inmates run the asylum.

A famous WELL anecdote concerns a young woman, a WELL regular, named Elly who decided to go to the Himalayas and become a Buddhist nun. She was breathing in and out for six months or so, had dropped off the WELL, and was almost forgotten, when she suddenly became ill with a dangerous liver ailment. Word was soon posted to the WELL that one of their own was in trouble (Elly had been hospitalized and was in a coma). The WELL regulars, which included doctors, travel agents—one of just about everything—mobilized quickly and efficiently, and arranged for Elly to be flown home.

Elly was cured, the WELL legend continues.

For those of you reading this who still aren't sure how a BBS differs from the larger Net, let me try to break down how it works:

On the Cellar, there is a local phone number, a suburban Philadelphia exchange (since that is where Tony lives). First, you set your computer to dial that number, and your modem makes a connection with one of the modems stacked in Tony Shepps's basement. The modems beep then make a horrible scratchy sound as if they are about to launch into space. The screen blinks a few times, you type in the command "bbs," then your name, and you are presented with a command-line menu that lets you do a number of things.

If you type "new" on the Cellar, you get instructions. If you type "cookie," as in fortune cookie, you get a pithy message, generated at random and often very funny. If you type "mail," you get your E-mail, if you have any. Most people on the Cellar type "boards" and read the various bulletin board topics.

On the Cellar, for instance, you can read messages posted to:

```
Board 100 Failsafe's Black Bag. Medicine and
  Related Topics.
Board 101 Philly Sports with Thom Darling.
Board 102 Aesch's Mathematics Board.
Board 103 Bears Auto Emporium.
```

```
Board 104 Toad's Wine Cellar.
Board 105 RichH's Memorial place. (Sex talk.)
Board 106 Bartz Political Zone.
Board 107 Trader's Zine Scene.
```

There are also boards for the discussion of books, movies, or computers, one with helpful tips on brewing beer, boards for gays and lesbians, a main board for the discussion of absolutely anything, and one for Extropians.

(What are Extropians? At first I figured they must be people who once lived in the tropics but have moved away. Later, I learned that the Extropians are a political group, basically Libertarian but more extreme, with an interest in cryonics and the technological extension of human intelligence. Go figure.)

Most everyone on the Cellar has their favorite board, many people read from and post to a number of boards, and a few brave souls read everything. (Frankly, I worry about them—the messages are not *that* interesting.) Each of these boards is like an intimate version of a Usenet group, like the bulletin board in my grocery store, only interactive. Anything goes. Some people are deadly serious no matter what the topic; some people can only crack wise.

According to folks at the barbecue, only one Cellar user ever offended enough people to merit discipline. He attacked everybody, they tell me, being simultaneously homophobic, separatist, and misogynistic. No, he wasn't a radio talk show host, but good guess.

No one could say a word without this guy jumping into the discussion, attacking, insulting, espousing viewpoints of which Hitler only dreamed. The Cellar's loyal users value the principle of free speech, however, and though most everyone soon grew sick of the offending voice, no one seemed ready to throw him off outright. (Yet it would have been quite easy—Tony could have just invalidated his account.)

Instead, in an E-mail conspiracy, they ignored him to death. If he advocated burning feminists at the stake, no one took the bait. If he suggested a separate African-American state, no one disagreed. If he championed the idea of boot camps for homo-sexuals, the idea went unacknowledged. He had the right to say it, but he couldn't get a rise out of anyone. He reportedly got bored—"Hey guys, don't you want to play anymore?"—and eventually went away.

Tony, the man who not only owns the Cellar but owns the cel-lar that holds the Cellar, is thirty, with dark hair, glasses, and a somewhat chagrined smile. He is a genial, generous host, spend-ing most of the GTG with smoke in his eyes, trying to cook enough chicken to feed a ravenous, fidgety crowd.

"There's a loose stereotype of people who like to interact with others by computer—we're supposed to be geeky, antisocial types who can't deal with live relationships," he tells me later. "These GTGs really disprove that image. Almost all of the regu-lar callers will eventually come to a GTG, and when they do, they're typically very social."

Tony refutes the notion that people who experience their social lives through a computer are retreating into shells. "We are *very* social—we tell stories, we ask for advice, we have secrets, we share concerns. So, when we get together, it feels natural and right to be social with each other, and so we are. We computer people are sometimes told to 'get a life'—I think this is actually a very nice part of a real life."

Tony makes no money off the Cellar. In fact, he loses money on a regular basis. He gives it away, actually. While those subscribers who want certain advanced features pay a small monthly fee, most subscribers, those who only want to read the Cellar's local boards, get their accounts for free. It is a word-of-mouth operation—Tony doesn't advertise. He lets anyone join and simply absorbs the costs of the equipment and phone lines. His wife rolls her eyes a lot. Tony is not a businessman, but he is a true lover of words and conversation, and he runs an extremely amicable, literate BBS.

He has wrestled, though, with the idea of making the Cellar bigger, better, and profitable. Even those Cellar subscribers who pay for advanced features can only toy around with two of the Internet's main tools (E-mail and Usenet.) The Internet has many other geegaws with names such as Archie, Veronica, Jughead, Gopher, ftp, and telnet—useful tools for searching on-line databases, contacting distant networks, or playing MUSH games. To use those features, Cellar dwellers need accounts with other service providers.

Admiring the Cellar's "community atmosphere," and no doubt its active base of users, a competing Internet provider in the Philadelphia area offered to grant Tony the software and Net connection necessary to make the Cellar a true Internet system. It would be a merger of sorts.

If Tony took his competitor up on the offer, and if he dug a deep trench into his neighbor's lawn to run some extra phone lines, a few things would happen:

1. More people would use the Cellar.
2. The neighbor would probably have a royal fit.
3. Tony might start making some money.

In his own inimitable, communal way, Tony went to the Cellar's current users to ask for opinions. "I have been thoroughly confused by all the possibilities," he confessed on the main message board. "Imagine if 50,000 people read a particular board, 400 people regularly posted messages to it, and there were all sorts of hit-and-run postings, anonymous postings. In general, you don't want to get to know the people on the other end of those messages. More often than not, you want them to come to physical harm.

"But if the Cellar could become an Internet hangout of sorts, with the kind of interplay we have, where we really get to know people, that would be interesting. It'd be interesting if one of our regular users was calling from Seattle, or England, or wherever."

Cellar loyalists quickly logged in with their responses, most of them sharing their host's fears of the Attack of the Internet Hordes, and some questioning the motives of the generous competitor. What really seemed to worry people was that the Cellar might get big and messy, and lose its intimacy.

Early into 1995, the Cellar remained a small, circumscribed system, and Tony was still weighing his options.

"I feel that it's generally better to do a few things very well," he explained, "than to do many things half-assed."

The Cellar's barbecue get-together dealt me a few surprises. I had expected awkward, ashen-faced computer junkies, and, well, okay, a few were there, but I was surprised by just how interesting they were, compared to my own preconceptions. I was, as I've said, also surprised by how well they could cook. I was surprised to find just how little equipment sat in Tony's basement, considering his BBS serves upward of 150 users. I was surprised that Tony was losing money in the midst of a gigantic Internet commercial boom. And I was surprised by how easily the straight males seemed to accept the Cellar's "transgendered" subculture.

Jerry Winner was the one who first tipped me off to the transgendered angle. Jerry is a young fellow, heavy with a dark beard, about to leave for the Baltimore area and a new job. "I was really shocked with the outpouring of sadness," he tells me, "because I didn't think I affected people that way. But I got about thirty messages from people saying 'I will really miss you' and 'keep in touch.' It's a big family thing."

He says he will probably continue to call into the Cellar, though it will now be long distance. "It's gotten to the point where I really like these people, and I don't want to lose that."

How, I ask him, does an on-line community differ from a face-to-face community?

"When you are on-line," Jerry theorizes, "you go a little bit farther, you're a little bit more frank and open. There are some things I would say on the Cellar that I would never say to my own friends. And a lot of times when you don't know what people look like you don't have the preconceptions about them. When you don't have anything to focus on, you just have to make judgments based on ideas and thoughts, and that's really cool."

I ask for an example.

"Well," he says, "for two years I thought Janice was a woman."

Janice is Mark. Or Mark is Janice.

In any case, Mark was born as Mark, but his on-line name is Janice, and some of his friends call him Janice, and some call him Mark. His wife is at the party. So are his daughters. They call him Dad.

Mark is not noticeably different from others in the room unless you take a close look. He has long, straight hair, but so do a lot of men. He has purple hoop earrings, though, really big ones, and a gold heart on a small chain. The heart is inscribed with his Net name, "Janice." He posts as Janice, always has, and unless you ran into him at a GTG, you would have no way to know that he is not a woman.

"The Cellar is a smaller space, and consequently more intimate," he says when I corner him for a chat. "You tend to have local folks on the Cellar and that gives it a unique flavor. It has culture and collective memory of its own. It's somewhat like a small town."

He is a computer programmer by day, and very personable. He enjoys the GTGs and seems amused that people are so astonished to find out what Janice really looks like. "I make no allusion to my birth gender on the Cellar."

Transgendered people are by definition those who want to live in a gender other than the one into which they were born—this includes cross-dressers, transvestites, and transsexuals. Transgendered people are fairly common on the Internet; it seems somewhat of a friendly magnet for them. "It was through CompuServe that I first discovered how many of us there were and how common it really was," Mark explains. "That was certainly a factor in my personal growth."

There is an organization known as TransgenderNet, a loose affiliation of BBSs that serve the transgendered community. Mark has served as a moderator on the cross-dressing section of TransgenderNet, and he says the anonymity offered by computer networks is very helpful to transgenderites. "A local psychologist said in a lecture to our support group, 'The first step in the process of coming out, admitting that you are in some way different, is coming out to yourself,' and these forums provide a place for this to occur without fear of rejection or censure."

Has he ever had a bad reaction from Cellar users?

"As a whole, they seem accepting. The people that hang out on the Cellar tend to be much less judgmental and a lot more open-minded. I guess it is the tone of the place. In general there is a tolerance for a broad range of viewpoints and kinds of people. Probably the only way you can get ostracized on the Cellar is to be intolerant. The one way you can gain censure is to be censorious yourself."

Mark points out Susan. Susan was once Fred, but she is a post-operative transsexual, which means now she is just Susan. She is blond, trim, husky-voiced, and she works in the same automotive tool-and-die shop she worked in before the operation. One day the guys in the shop just hung up a banner reading, GOODBYE FRED, HELLO SUSAN.

Sometimes the world is a marvelous place.

"I personally seem to have a tough time just meeting people," Susan confides. "Always have. Computer networking is an anonymous way of meeting people ahead of time, so you can kinda pick and choose who you might actually meet."

This is her first GTG, and she is finding the folks to be friendly. "I think we all kinda feel we know each other to a certain extent."

Like Mark, Susan allows that the Internet played a key role in her gender journey. "The Cellar gave me access to the Internet and to a rather private kind of area. It was through the Internet that I chose the surgeon to do the surgery. I was able to do an enormous amount of research."

That was another useful use for the Net that came up again and again as I was writing this book: it is a great place to ask questions you might be embarrassed to flat-out ask someone face-to-face.

Susan also likes the ability to tell people about herself from a distance. "You can tell people anonymously. You're not committing yourself to someone who might not take it the right way. If someone doesn't take it the right way, it's easy to ignore them. It gives you a real nice way to find out—whatever it might be, on any subject—how it's going to go."

"So you like the Net?" I ask.

She laughs, a big, hearty, genuine laugh. "I think it's just great. Hey, what can I say?"

chapter seven

THE ZIPPO CHAPTER

The Net Gets Inflammatory

Thoreau once wrote, "For my part, I could easily do without the post office. I never received more than one or two letters in my life . . . that were worth the postage."

Well, that was long before the mail became electronic and postage became almost obsolete, but once again, the cabin-dwelling ascetic raises an interesting question. With all of these words rushing up and down, to and fro, back and forth, with thousands of messages crossing the Net on a daily basis, is any of it worth reading?

Thoreau had high standards, of course. In his day, letters could take weeks or months to reach their destination, and it was not entirely improbable that the correspondents might spend nearly as much time in composition. Back when Thoreau was just a budding Transcendentalist looking for a small body of water and some solitude, many passionate relationships were conducted by mail. Letter writing was considered a high form of art, and the printed word was precious.

These days?

Ouch.

The Net is a wonderful place where freedom of speech is preeminent. There are no censors to speak of, and no editors either. It is the world's largest magazine, and we are all unpaid guest writers with free rein. What goes out, goes out whenever the author deems his words ready for public consumption, or perhaps when his finger brushes the send button inadvertently. In all too many cases, the author is clearly not his own best critic.

So how bad is it?

"Writing on the Net is as good as you can expect, considering how densely loaded it is with people whose main intimate relationship is with their computers," Jack Mingo jokes. He should know—Mingo is the author of over nine books, and a celebrated regular on the Usenet group misc.writing, where writers discuss the nuts and bolts of publication, complain about rejections, and play an endless series of word games while getting over cases of writer's block. "As in everything," Mingo says, "eighty percent of the writing on the Net is boring, ten percent is maddening in its wrongheadedness, and ten percent is brilliant and entertaining and makes slogging through the rest of it worthwhile."

Mingo is one of those who do it well. His postings to misc.writing and his E-mail messages are short, to the point, witty, and usually fit on one screen. Screen size is a real limitation on the Internet. Depending on your software, a certain key will let you jump up and down the electronic page display, but in my experience, the herky-jerkiness of electronic reading makes anything more than few paragraphs seem tedious and unpleasant. Reading colored blips on a screen will never, in my humble opinion, replace the good feel of a thick book.

But people *are* writing. I ask Mingo if this simple fact, all these folks scribbling messages late into the night instead of watching television, might eventually make better writers out of us? Will the printed (or posted) word suddenly become important again?

"There is an irony here," he responds. "In the same way the 'paperless office' has turned out to be anything but, the 'post-literate computer era' has become one in which the outdated form of words on a neutral background has become dominant."

But the writing has changed from the days of epistolary eloquence, Mingo concedes. Words may not have their same value.

"It is a different kind of medium, because there is no illusion of writing something for the ages. Unlike even correspondence—where you can at least imagine that the recipient of your letters is saving them and that they might be published posthumously after you become famous—writing on the Net is like making sandcastles. You know that no matter how much care you put into the process, it will all be washed away after a while. In many ways it is like cocktail party conversation. The most you can hope for is that it will make an impression before it disappears into the air."

This ephemerality, the transitory nature of Net writing, is made worse by a simple reality of the marketplace. Many of the large access providers, the middlemen who connect single computer users to the greater Internet world, charge these users by the hour or allow only a certain number of hours per month for a basic fee. Thoreau, of course, could pinch a penny until the darned thing turned black and blue, so perhaps he would sympathize with the average Net correspondent, the poor guy hunched over his computer at bedtime (when rates are lowest), composing E-mail and Usenet postings as fast as his stubby fingers can poke the keyboard, trying to cram as much activity as possible into five hours a month. Perhaps Thoreau would sympathize, but then he never had to read this stuff.

The time factor is part of the problem (though this is mitigated somewhat by new programs that allow you to read and respond to messages "off-line," when the meter isn't running), but another factor is simple sloppiness. I teach writing, spend more than a few hours each week evaluating essays written by college freshmen, and am a frontline witness to the decline of spelling, grammar, and basic sentence construction. In a few years, I will be an old crank.

Like my colleagues in English departments across the country, I blame television. You don't learn to spell, see where the comma should go, or recognize basic sentence patterns unless you read, and my students don't read anything. More than a few react to the assignment of writing a simple five-paragraph essay as if I had asked for seven stanzas of iambic pentameter.

Well, the writing on the Net reminds me too often of the writing of my poorest students, only worse. People don't just misspell words, they ignore the conventions of spelling entirely. Sentences are not misconstructed, they are not constructed at all.

Moreover, much of it is simply lifeless. Your average attempt at a poem posted to the Net resembles the following:

> Every time i think of u,
> My heart feels deep emotion,
> And if you ever leave me girl,
> i'll jump into the deepest ocean . . .

By and large, the short stories are worse: rehashed parables, bad Stephen King imitations, and indecipherable streams of consciousness.

To quote Thoreau again, "the man whose horse trots a mile in a minute does not carry the most important message," and surely the Net's much-touted speediness of conveyance does not in any way improve content. Too many Usenet postings and E-mail letters look like Western Union telegrams composed by fourth graders: "Dont like your idea at all . . . you dum ass . . . wat where you thinking! . . . ? . . . you otta get a clue man, or noone will ever take yur ideas seriously!"

Oh, by the way, that last bit was a flame. An honest-to-goodness flame.

People on and off the Net seem fascinated by the whole phenomenon of flaming. Page after page has been written about this in newspapers and magazines over the last year, as if flaming were a serious social problem. Knowing the word "flame" has come to be seen as evidence that you understand everything there is to know about electronic communication.

Flaming is when someone, usually someone you don't know and never will, sends you a rude, insulting, often obscene message, either as a response within a Usenet newsgroup or directly to your electronic mailbox. They do this, I assume, to get their giggles, and because there are no repercussions. The flamer might be in New Zealand. You aren't likely to track him down and punch his nose.

A well-composed, G-rated flame, for example, might sound something like this:

> You pea-brained idiot. You total imbecile. I wouldn't wash my floor with your face if you were the last mop in the closet. You stupid moron. You ignoramus. Bite me.

I have a friend, a young woman who is basically intelligent in most other aspects, who told me with a straight face that she would never, ever get a Net account because "I am afraid I might get flamed."

She was serious. This really worried her.

Well here is what I suggested:

Find a Zippo lighter. Hold it in your left hand. Pretend you are G. Gordon Liddy, the spook who completely bungled the Watergate break-in and somehow became an American patriot, and hold your right hand momentarily over the flame.

Did that hurt?

Sure.

Now try this:

Have a friend who is forty miles away light a Zippo, then ask him to type the words, "I am holding the lighter right under your hand," on his computer.

Did you feel that?

Of course not. And that's the way I feel about flames. Sticks and stones may break my bones, but flames, at worst, can only break my concentration.

At best, they break me up.

But let's say you *really* don't want to get flamed. To some, I'm told, a flame can be as offensive as an obscene phone call, coming out of nowhere, catching you off-guard. The fact that the flaming message appears right on your "personal" computer can seem like a violation of privacy, an intrusion into your home.

Well, to be brief, you probably attracted the flame either of two ways. First, you may have disagreed on-line with someone who listens to Rush Limbaugh. This is a good way to get horribly flamed, so just ignore them when you see them. Second, and most likely, you probably violated one of the basic rules of "Netiquette" (a clever shorthand for Net Etiquette).

To keep you safe in the future, then, here are:

The Basic Rules of Netiquette

1) Read the FAQ.

This is a great rule, except lots of people don't know what it means. FAQ is short for Frequently Asked Questions, a document that most serious groups post every week or two. FAQs list not only those questions that come up frequently in the group (why does my cat sleep with the toilet brush?), but also the answers. This is to avoid repetition. Repetition is a particular problem on Usenet because so many new people discover it every day, and they all have the same queries. Otherwise, to flog the superhighway metaphor, it would be like trying to drive home from work while thousands of pimply sixteen-year-old boys attempt to pull you over and ask, "What's the turn signal do, dude?" If you have a question, the correct etiquette is to see if it is in the FAQ before posting the question and wasting everyone's time and electricity. There is also an all-encompassing FAQ called Frequently Asked Questions about Usenet that can be found in news.announce.newusers.

2) Lurk Before You Post.

Mother always taught me to look both ways before crossing the street. And to never eat food off the floor. In case you are reading, Mom, I will say here that I have never wavered. Similarly, the self-appointed Emily Post Etiquette Cops on Usenet repeatedly insist that a new user should lurk (read a newsgroup, but not say anything) for two entire weeks before even considering the idea of posting a question or an answer. I have never followed this rule, by the way. It doesn't suit my nature.

3) Don't Use All Caps.

It is considered a very bad idea to use all capital letters in your Usenet postings or in E-mail, because certain people have decided it is JUST LIKE SHOUTING. To be honest, I have no idea WHY it is just like shouting, since it makes no noise, but people treat it that way. Sometimes, it seems to me, you just want some EMPHASIS. But seriously, if you DO IT, you might get FLAMED!!

4) Don't Say Anything Stupid.

But that is relative, right? And if intelligence were a prerequisite for admission to the Internet, why would there be a Usenet group called alt.bitch.pork?

And finally:

5) Write Briefly, Be Clear.

A good rule speaks for itself.

chapter eight

SPAM, SPAM, SPAM, AND SPAM
Doing Business on the Net

If the narrow electronic footpath called the Internet is ever going to become an Amazing Information Superhighway, if the existing network of university and corporate computers is ever going to become more than just a dust and dirt road, then it will be due to people such as Peter Berger, hot behind the wheel of his big green cement truck.

Though, as I've said, there *is* no real Superhighway at the moment, portions of the roadbed are being cleared and graded, and Berger's truck, with a massive whirling bucket and Telerama, Inc., printed on the side, is rushing in with a load of wet concrete.

And if the truck doesn't break down, as this metaphor surely will any second now, Telerama will soon have paved its own small section of the larger road.

Despite my metaphorical fabrication, Peter Berger doesn't look at all like a truck driver: no dangling cigarette, no Peterbilt cap, not much in the way of whiskers. He doesn't look that much like an attorney, either, though he is one, general counsel to Luce McQuillen Corp. He is also system administrator for Telerama, Inc., Pittsburgh's first local access provider.

While Tony Shepps's Cellar, a bulletin board system, exists mainly to offer its own discussion groups, Telerama's primary purpose is to hook people into the Internet. There are hundreds of local access providers like Telerama, with more starting up every day; for people who want to be on the Internet but don't have a free account at work or school, these local providers tend to offer a better Internet price than major national services such as Prodigy and CompuServe, though the latter offer more in the way of features.

On the day we are to meet, I fully expect to find Berger in one of those glass and steel towers that forest Pittsburgh's golden triangle—there is something so decidedly corporate about the name Luce McQuillen Corp. But instead, Berger's office is housed in a nondescript brick building, up a steep stairwell, behind a door that doesn't even have a sign.

The angled building, otherwise empty, fits tightly into the irregular hills of Mount Washington, a few short blocks from the Monongahela Incline. It is a modest neighborhood, to be generous. The morning I visit, the street is empty except for a few elderly men in shorts and dark socks shouting their impressions of the two-run Orlando Merced double that helped the Pirates squeak past the Florida Marlins the evening before.

General counsel? I expect Berger to be pin-striped, buttoned-down, and graying at the temples. My own preconception of lawyers, I suppose. The fact is, Berger looks like my nephew.

Though he is twenty-five, the Brooklyn native appears younger, barely out of college—much less law school. He has short, dark hair, a friendly round face, glasses, and enough energy for six. Berger has forgone the expected Brooks Brothers suit for blue jeans, a black T-shirt, and purple Converse high-top sneakers.

He is an Internet zealot, it turns out, spending almost every minute of the workday logged on. His own introduction to the Internet world went like this:

After graduating from Pitt Law School, Berger worked for Legal Aid in Washington, Pennsylvania, specializing in divorce and child custody, but his friends Doug and Todd (aka Luce and McQuillen) wanted to open Telerama, and they needed Berger's advice.

"So I went to my boss and said, 'Hey I'd like to do some work on the side,' and he said, 'No, you can't do that.' So I told Doug that if he wanted me, he would have to offer me a real job, so they offered me a real job and I jumped."

Berger keeps Telerama running, clearing clogged files, answering phones, answering electronic mail. What this means is that he gets to play on the computer all day long, and he fairly loves it.

"When I worked for Legal Aid, I couldn't wait to get out of there. Now I don't even notice when five o'clock rolls around." He says it isn't work, but fun. "Anytime you want, you can blow off and read news, or E-mail your friends."

Berger cradles a keyboard on his lap almost the whole time we talk. Our morning is interrupted again and again by a ringing phone—Telerama customers with frozen screens or garbled messages—but Berger handles the calls quickly and sends the callers on their merry ways. He laughs a lot and looks at the ceiling whenever someone phones him with a senseless or rudimentary question.

But Berger's demeanor changes the moment I ask about legal issues. He invisibly switches hats, and now I see the attorney-at-law. "The big issue, for an access provider, is liability," he explains, sitting up in his leather recliner. "There is no quick fix to that. There's no way to just make people sign a document and all of a sudden we aren't liable. People can use our system for any number of things. If they wanted to—it's against our rules—but if they wanted, they could conceivably log on and use it for drug transactions or conspiring to murder someone or any number of bad things. Now, are we liable for that?"

His is not the only company worrying about such liability, by the way. Prodigy, which is owned by Sears, runs software that automatically searches out obscene words and then removes the offending messages from its bulletin boards. America Online has had to take action to remove alleged child pornographers from its service.

A bank of modems whines and whistles in the back room, a signal that more people are calling in and getting connected. My eyes come to rest on a bottle of Tums near Berger's terminal. I ask if the antacid tablets belong to him.

"Yes," he laughs. "But I think it's a really good sign that the bottle has been here for two months."

Telerama and other access providers inhabit a gray area in the communications industry. Phone companies, Berger explains, are designated by the government as "common carriers" and, as such, are not liable for a customer's misuse. "But the phone company gives up a whole lot of rights in terms of their pricing in order to get that immunity. Some businesses in our position are sort of claiming, 'Oh, we're a common carrier.' Now, I feel like we're a common carrier, we act like a common carrier, but there is a question of whether legally we really are. If someone ever did something, could we be legally sued? That's the problem that's giving me gray hairs."

I still don't see the gray, but I can see the concern. "What else?" I ask.

Berger sets aside the keyboard, pulls his plush executive chair to the rim of his semicirclar desk. "There are some ethical questions," he says. "We value our customers' privacy. We assure them that we don't go poking around in their stuff, but what happens if someone tells us, 'So and so is doing this'? This happens all the time. People say, 'So and so is doing something bad, go stop them.' At what point do we have the right, or the obligation, to go in and actually take an action? We try to be as laissez-faire as possible."

I ask Berger to be specific, to give an example of a misbehaving customer, but the lawyer is cautious. So I ask for a composite, a hypothetical.

"Well, suppose one of our woman customers comes to us and says, 'Okay, this man customer over here is stalking me. He sends me E-mail messages every day that are lewd and lascivious and I'm beginning to think a little threatening. He's sending me talk requests all the time. Whenever I get on IRC [an Internet feature that allows people to "chat" in real time, much as they might on a CB radio,] he follows me around and sends me messages. He called me at home the other night.' What do we do in a situation like this? One, we can do nothing. Two, we suggest to the woman some ways to alleviate the situation, such as setting things up so that E-mail he sends her will bounce.''

(Bouncing is the computer version of "return to sender," and it can be set up to work automatically so that any mail from one particular address is not accepted at another particular address. The mail just bounces back to the sender. These bounce arrangements involve some computer programming, but can be executed by a reasonably adept professional or advanced hobbyist.)

Berger continues:

"Moving up a rung, we can send him a message saying, 'You know what you are doing is really uncool and we think you should stop.' Or we can send him a message saying, 'You are being really uncool and if you continue this behavior we're going to kick you off the system.' A fifth option would be to go and turn him into the cops. There is a whole spectrum of responses we can take. But which one should we take? What's a principled way of responding?"

Berger and Telerama, Inc., are in the electronic culture business itself, but much more hotly contested, and just as legally unclear, is the question of how this culture might help, or harm, businesses of other sorts. Everyone seems to have a different idea about what this new electronic turnpike should become; yet one thing seems certain: the Information Superhighway has tremendous business potential, and getting in on the ground floor now might be as lucrative as was securing Atlanta's first cable franchise or owning exclusive rights to manufacture microwave popcorn.

This potential to make money has become its own Internet controversy, right alongside censorship and pornography, generating massive arguments and more flames than the entire lifetime output of the Zippo plant. In fact, using the Net to post advertising is considered by many to be a shameless breach of net etiquette, and those who follow, fret over, and frequently flame net abusers even have their own newsgroup, alt.current-events.net-abuse.

The best-known example of alleged Net abuse is a series of postings by two Phoenix lawyers, Laurence A. Canter and Martha S. Siegel. The lawyers, a married couple, posted an advertisement in April 1994 to thousands of Usenet newsgroups, everything from misc.fitness to rec.arts.disney. Sending a posting to more than one group in this way is known as crossposting. Sending to a multitude of groups is known as a spam, after a famously repetitious Monty Python comedy sketch. Canter and Siegel, as their notoriety increases on the Internet, are often simply referred to as Crosspost & Spam by their detractors.

The lawyers' simple ad raised hackles for a number of reasons. One seems to have been that people on the Internet don't like lawyers any more than people elsewhere. The second reason is that the ad, an offer to help immigrants participate in the federal government's green card lottery, was seen by their critics as a scam, and perhaps a ruthless one, since the lawyers were charging a fee to help aliens fill out forms for what was meant to be a free lottery. The final reason is that the crossposting to literally thousands of unrelated Usenet groups was seen as a new form of electronic junk mail: it was not related to any topic normally discussed on the newsgroups, nobody had apparently asked for the information, yet it filled countless electronic mailboxes.

What really bothered people was not that Canter and Siegel did this once (or even that they went on to repeat it again), but the thought of what would happen if other people started to do it, too, if the firm's innovative electronic advertising strategy worked out and innumerable companies, large and small, jumped on the bandwagon.

You see, this ability to spam, to reach millions of readers sitting in front of millions of machines, is, unlike conventional junk mail, basically *free*, aside from the cost of an access account. Name another way to reach millions of potential customers at such a price. Short of jumping off a tall building with advertising on your T-shirt, there aren't many. With a little technical knowledge, I could spam, you could spam, every charity and mail-order shoe company on the planet could spam, and what would that do to the Internet itself? Would it change the basic character of the Net—the hopeful, forward-looking, free-speech frontier mentality? Would it drive people away? Would the whole thing just explode?

People went to a lot of trouble to make sure that Canter and Siegel's crossposting strategy did not work, everything from filling the firm's return electronic mailbox with flames and junk so that no legitimate replies could get through, to notifying various state bar associations of the firm's conduct and alleging that it was improper, to writing complicated programs called cancel-bots that automatically erased subsequent Canter and Siegel postings moments after they appeared.

Others took thousands of those little subscription cards that fall out of magazines and filled them out with Martha Siegel's name and address. Following the green card lottery post, Ms. Siegel told *The Wall Street Journal* that she received "carloads" of magazines to which she had never subscribed.

And others simply took to the Net: denouncing the pair, calling for retaliation or legislation, protecting their home turf. The argument has been going on for over a year now, and shows no signs of stopping.

Canter and Siegel themselves continue to practice law. They have published their own book (*How to Make a Fortune on the Information Superhighway*), claim to have generated about $100,000 in business from the ad (though others dispute this), and have set up their own Internet marketing agency to help other companies distribute commercial messages.

Was what Canter and Siegel did illegal? Not at all. Basically, nothing is illegal on the Internet unless it is illegal off the Internet: for example, threatening the president, transmitting child pornography, or engaging in securities fraud.

Was what Canter and Siegel did unethical? Well, that depends on whose ethics you want to consider. The American Bar Association for instance, fully permits its members to advertise.

I posted a request to the aforementioned newsgroup, alt.current-events.net-abuse, asking what was so onerous about the

Canter and Siegel green card incident, and received numerous replies within hours, many of them pages long.

Adam Elman, a graduate student in computer science at Stanford University, pointed out that many magazine and newspaper articles on the Crosspost & Spam affair had missed the point:

> The issue with the Green Card post and other
> spams has NOT been advertising. There are
> those who feel any advertising on the Net is
> wrong; however, they're really living in the
> past. Advertising on the Net is inevitable.
> The problem with C&S, pure & simple, is that
> they misused Usenet. Not by posting an adver-
> tisement, but by posting an advertisement to
> a wide variety of newsgroups to which the
> post was irrelevant. Usenet is based on the
> idea of the newsgroup; if I want to read
> articles about Mac communications, I read
> comp.sys.mac.comm; if I want to read articles
> about current episodes of Star Trek, I read
> rec.arts.startrek.current. I don't expect
> to see advertisements about the Green Card
> lottery in the Star Trek group.

Mitchell Golden, an assistant professor of physics at Harvard, echoed Elman:

> What Canter and Siegel did was to flood every
> Usenet newsgroup with copies of their "Green

Card ad". For example, here at Harvard it
showed up in private university newsgroups,
such as harvard.course.phys15c — which is supposed to be used to distribute course materials
to students. This is, as even Mr. Canter and
Ms. Siegel surely know, an abuse of the system.
The objection to the immigration lawyers'
posts isn't their commercial content. Usenet
readers just want them in the right newsgroup:
alt.visa.us.

Another reply, from Tom Ritchford of New York City,
summed it up quite colorfully:

Imagine that you are sitting in a cafe, talking to a few friends. Then, someone comes in
with a megaphone and proceeds to deliver an
advertisement, in fact an advertisement that
is trying to sell for $75 something that you
can get for free. You later discover that
this individual has done this in every cafe
in the city . . . and that this individual
intends to do this repeatedly.

Only two people weighed in on the other side. One of them
was Charles Packer, a programmer working at NASA's Goddard
Space Flight Center, who wrote, "I maintain that Usenet should
continue to be an adventure in absolute freedom of speech and be
open to whatever anyone wants to post. Net etiquette may be that
advertisements are not to be posted, and this should be sufficient
to dissuade potential advertisers because of inevitable ill-will."

The other was from Sue D. Nym, a clever pseudonym. Sue wrote this: "Frankly, I don't think what C&S did was worth the uproar it generated. The response was like 'mob justice' and 'vigilantism.' The Internet is far less civilized than the world understands."

There are other "spam" advertisers, of course, though less notorious. For instance, you can buy Tupperware on the Net. You can even host an electronic gathering, and "earn hostess gifts just like you would at a regular Tupperware party." Others have spam-advertised Miracle Thigh Creme, incense, herbal diet plans, and various get-rich-quick schemes. Authors have even plugged their own books.

And, of course, businesses are finding new (and less upsetting) ways to use the Internet as fast as you can read this page. A few of the larger mail-order personal computer retailers have their own Usenet groups—a handy way to answer technical support questions, and not a bad way to keep your name in front of the customer in a low-key way. On-line shopping catalogs for everything from clothing to fruit are appearing on the Internet almost as fast as those old-fashioned paper catalogs appear in the mailbox at your curb. A California nightclub uses the Net to post a listing of upcoming bands, and more than a few restaurants have begun posting menus, with updated daily specials. A new part of the Net called the World Wide Web—which I'll examine at length later—is bursting with business and advertising.

The lesson for the Net's architects, I suppose, is this:

When it comes to advertisers and the Net—If you build it, they will come.

• • •

Should you by chance be thinking of opening your own local access provider, you will be pleased to know that it doesn't take all that much in the way of equipment. Peter Berger's outfit occupies just two small rooms. There is a third room, to be honest, with a conference table and refrigerator, but it doesn't look as if it has seen much use. Berger holds court in the front room with his desk, his computer, and a small sofa for clients. The back room houses a few personal computers, a bank of twenty-eight standard modems, a laser printer, shelves of what seem like spare parts, and one exotic piece of hardware: an SMSDU (Switched Multimegabit Data Service Unit). People phone Telerama from home or business and connect in with one of the standard modems, the modem connects with the SMSDU, and the SMSDU connects to the rest of the Internet, transmitting data at a very fast 1.17 megabytes per second.

Of course, you need to know how to set all these devices up and work the software that lets them talk. That's where Doug and Todd come in.

Telerama started as Chat Thing, a bulletin board system not unlike the Cellar. "Todd [McQuillen] had used one of these in Chicago and when he came to Pittsburgh he really missed it," Berger told me. "So his wife, as a wedding present, bought him six phone lines."

Doug Luce, the other partner, owned a bit of sophisticated equipment for UNIX (the hardware and software system that provides the Internet's basic technical vocabulary) and "it just sort of mutated over time. We had the advantage of doing this at a time that really no one else was doing it. So we've been able to grow as the hype grows."

Pittsburgh now has a handful of local access providers and a FreeNet (yet another wrinkle—a no-cost provider), with others in the works, but Berger isn't worried. "We think the FreeNet is going to be a good thing, because it will get more people interested in the Internet in general."

In the summer of 1994, Telerama had five hundred customers, and was growing, in Berger's own words, "rapidly."

How rapidly?

"I used to think that the main market was expatriate college students, people who have lost their college accounts. But the people we are getting on-line now are very unsophisticated as far as computers are concerned. They are just people who said, 'You know what, this sounds really neat and I would like to do it.' A lot of retirees, a lot of married couples. So obviously the market is a lot bigger than we originally thought."

Just how big is it?

Berger laughs, asks me when my book will come out. He doesn't want to encourage competition.

So we leave it at this:

The greater Pittsburgh area, the locals who might want local access, is home to roughly 2 million people, and multiplying that by twenty dollars a month would buy a lot of processed pork shoulder.

The Net, like it or not, is fast becoming big business, and many business people are only just starting to catch on. Get your cement trucks ready. Once the Internet marketers figure out how to make this all work, the term "cash flow" is going to take on a whole new meaning.

chapter nine

WHY WE PAY OUR CIVIL SERVANTS SO MUCH MONEY

Government by Inter-Newt

In my quest to unearth some deeper truth about our electronic culture, my adventure in detaching fact from fancy, perhaps the only claim I heard more often than the one about how our interpersonal relationships will be forever transformed was the one about how our democratic form of government will be radically altered. Barely a day would pass without my reading a magazine article or Usenet posting announcing in no uncertain terms that the Net was absolutely, decisively, and positively going to turn Washington upside down and inside out. Thanks to electronic mail and many other inventive ways and means of swapping information through phone lines, the nation's democratic process was soon to become an open book, accessible, convenient to all, and as wonderfully efficient as a Pizza Hut! (I'll take welfare reform with extra cheese, thank you.)

The Government Transformation Forecast goes like this: our representatives in Washington have to this point been a distant, privileged, inaccessible elite who listen only to the pleasing *rip rip rip* sounds emanating from the fatcat lobbyists' checkbooks. But soon—once you, and I, and every loyal citizen with a modem and a keyboard begin forcefully and instantaneously telling our congresspeople, our senators, and even president@ whitehouse.gov what we think, what we want, and when we want it—the direction of our nation will be firmly in our hands—safe, secure, just the way Thomas Jefferson originally intended.

Sounds good, but is it true?

I'll give you three guesses.

The federal government *is* using E-mail big time; in fact almost every office in our nation's capital is linked to almost every other office, and increasingly these offices are being linked to the outside, to the public, to us. We can, indeed, send E-mail to the White House on any issue, from term limits to our neighbor's annoying habit of dumping lawn clippings in the street.

And many, both within and without the government, seem convinced that this greater access will lead to greater involvement on the part of We the People, more accountability on the part of our elected officials, and a more Jeffersonian, more responsive, more productive, more perfect union. In a progress report entitled "Technology for Economic Growth," President Clinton himself promised that this new information technology will dramatically improve the way the federal government serves the people.

Well, I have my doubts, as I've indicated, especially when it

comes to elected representatives and the entrenched bureaucracy that helps them accomplish so little. Wanting to know
more about these improvements in service, I used my own considerable influence and sweet-talked myself into a visit with the
techno-bureaucrats who operate the House E-mail network. We
rendezvoused one Thursday on an upstairs floor of the dismal
but charmingly bulky Gerald R. Ford House Office Building.
The people I met were exceedingly nice, well informed, and wore
more powerful power ties than I personally have ever worn.
Before they even spoke, however, it was made clear that I could
not, under any circumstances short of torture, reveal to you their
names.

I can tell you the name of their boss at the time, Charlie Rose,
Democrat-NC, chairman of the Committee on House Admin-
istration before the New Republicans took over; but I can't tell
you who they are. A Rose by any other name, you see, would get
these bureaucrats in trouble.

I was told that this is a standard rule in Washington, though
it is nowhere written down. When reporters refer to "House
sources," this is what they mean. They mean the men and
women who do all the work but aren't up for reelection every
few years and don't really need the publicity.

"It's the way the Hill works," the senior bureaucrat told me.
"All the credit goes to the representatives."

Wowza, I thought. *I'm in the Halls of Power now.*

The House sources I met, *my* House sources, are responsible
for every congressperson's electronic mail link and, for that matter, for the E-mail going in and out, down and through all the
offices that serve our splendidly recompensed elected officials.

As part of this responsibility, they oversee the United States House of Representatives Constituent Electronic Mail System.

All House offices have access to internal electronic mail, and last year they were sending messages back and forth at a dizzying rate of 6,066 a day, but by early 1995 only about forty House members also had "public mailboxes," open to the voters. For instance, georgia6@hr.house.gov is Newt Gingrich, and if you send Newt Gingrich a message, the Constituent Electronic Mail System is what responds.

Neat, huh? You can E-mail Newt Gingrich.

Except we are talking about Washington, right? And nothing is simple in Washington. If you send electronic mail to Newt or anyone else, what you will get back is a rapid electronic form letter from an auto-responder. An auto-responder is a bit of software sorcery that receives your message, takes note of your return address, and responds, all with no human intervention. Think of it as a robotic federal clerk that, thankfully, has no need for healthcare or dental benefits.

The auto-response begins like this:

```
Thank you for contacting me through the House
of Representatives Constituent Electronic Mail
System (CEMS). I am pleased to be a part of
this effort to offer citizens a quick and effi-
cient way to communicate with the representa-
tives in Congress.
```

Quick and efficient is really a matter of opinion, however. The auto-response is certainly quick, taking as few as five seconds on a slow mail day; but that's it, electronically speaking.

If you come from the representative's home district, then maybe three or four months down the line someone might read your message and the massive federal Information SuperLogJam will send you, through the U.S. Mail, another letter, saying, "Though the representative doesn't necessarily agree with your views on sending convicted criminals to live 20,000 Leagues Under the Sea, he has voted many times to stiffen criminal penalties and he greatly values your opinions."

This bears repeating: the electronic mail we send our representatives gets answered *through the U.S. Postal Service*, that behemoth of a bureaucracy that E-mail is supposed to gloriously sidestep. On the very day I met with my House sources, in fact, *The Washington Post* reported that the D.C. area had "the worst mail service in the nation." Postal inspectors had found undelivered mail in one post office that was over five months late.

"Of course to the Internet gurus," my House source explains, "this is blasphemy."

And did you notice the second catch? Representatives will only respond if you come from their home district.

My highly placed House source explains that as well. "The internal rules are such that representatives cannot be responding to a constituent not in their district, because if they did that it would be considered electioneering."

Electioneering means canvassing for votes, and representatives can only canvas for votes at home; otherwise they are stepping on some other representative's toes, or running for president. We wouldn't want that either, would we?

Well, maybe not in Newt's case.

. . .

Over at the Senate, on the other hand, I found a source who was willing to be named. Chris Casey, Technology Policy Advisor to Senator Edward M. Kennedy, is a bit of an internet guru in the federal system. Among other things, he has a really neat picture of the U.S. Capitol attached to the bottom of all his outgoing E-mail messages.

Casey estimates that maybe twelve Senators have public mailboxes. Unlike the House, however, which maintains a list of addresses that can be obtained via E-mail, Casey explained that no public list existed of E-mail addresses for Senators.

I don't mean to sound rude, or maybe I do, but really, if the addresses aren't publicly available, they are hardly public, are they? I love Washington. People in Washington make Groucho Marx seem logical.

Senator Kennedy does have a *public* public mailbox though, (senator@kennedy.senate.gov), and his office is clearly at the forefront of computer networking. And yes, I know that a lot of people would like to hear Senator Kennedy jokes here, but I happen to like the senator, and you have all heard the jokes anyway, so just insert them here yourself.

So, what is Kennedy doing with the Net?

"In May of 1993," Casey explained, "Senator Kennedy's office began posting the senator's press releases and statements to a small network of computer bulletin boards in Massachusetts and providing users the means to comment electronically. Thanks to assistance from the Artificial Intelligence Lab at Massachusetts Institute of Technology, these same materials were also posted to two Usenet newsgroups (ne.politics, talk.politics.misc) and were kept at an ftp archive at MIT. When the senate Internet sites became available, we began to also post the same materials to them."

He had more to say, but I found myself distracted by a simple question: if the Internet only gives us greater access to our elected officials' press releases and public statements, and not to our elected officials, how the hell is it going to change the world?

And then there is the White House. Despite repeated attempts, I could get no one at the White House to talk with me about their use of the Internet and electronic mail, even when I mentioned that I thought Bob Dole looked remarkably like Doctor Strangelove. But, then, who could blame them. It seems these days that whenever the White House talks to anyone about anything, a special prosecutor is appointed.

Here, though, is what I do know about the White House:

1. They do have public electronic mail addresses:
   —president@whitehouse.gov
   —vice-president@whitehouse.gov
   —socks-the-cat@whitehouse.gov
2. It is unclear who reads the E-mail. Maybe the cat.

But it is neat to send messages to the White House, and fun to tell your friends. I sent the following, for instance:

```
Date: 15 August 1994, 11:11:54 EDT
From: D. W. Moore
```

```
Subject: Lawn Clippings
To: president@whitehouse.gov
```

Dear Sir,

My neighbor, Ed, repeatedly, throughout the
summer, has been dumping his lawn clippings off
the curb and onto the street in front of his
home. When it rains, these clippings wash down
to my curb, where they create an unsightly and
dangerous green goo-like substance. My local
township officials have no interest in solving
this problem, so I am appealing to you. Could
legislation be sponsored that would make this a
federal crime? Or could you call Ed? He voted
for you, and respects your opinion.

> Thank you,
> D. W. Moore

And, yes, they actually answered.

The auto-responder, concerned and responsive as always,
considered my query for three-quarters of an hour, then sent
back this reassuring note:

```
Date: Mon, 15 Aug 94 11:57:35
From: autoresponder@whitehouse.gov
Subject: Re: Lawn Clippings
To: D. W. Moore
```

Thank you for writing to President Clinton
via electronic mail. Since June 1993, white-
house.gov has received over 250,000 messages
from people all over the world.

        Although the volume of mail prevents the Presi-
        dent from personally reviewing each message, the
        mail is read by White House staff. Your concerns,
        ideas, and suggestions are carefully recorded
        and communicated to the President weekly with a
        representative sampling of the mail.

Of course, if you include your street address in your message to the White House, you may eventually receive a personalized response by U.S. Mail. A crack team of epistolary scribes has drafted a dizzying array of form letters that vaguely address any issue we can raise, and one of these form letters will be picked out of a computer file, printed on White House stationery, and sent your way within mere weeks.

Do you see how E-mail is changing everything?

Even though our elected officials are eager to use the Internet to send public policy pronouncements and thrilling notices of their day-to-day accomplishments to various Usenet groups and electronic mailing lists, it is beginning to seem clear that they have this problem with the messages we send them. To be blunt, they treat electronic mail from you and me, the loyal and blameless voters, as if it were the badly soiled diaper of a radioactive child.

Why?

Actually, there are some good reasons.

The folks in Washington are very concerned about what is called "spoof" mail. By this they don't mean imbecilic morons who send dumb but essentially harmless messages about lawn clippings, they mean people who send harmful messages. There are a few scenarios, and they are very real and very possible.

"Security is a big problem," my House source explained, "in and out. Every which way. Who is sending? Who is responding? Where does the mail really come from?"

If I knew more about computers, basic stuff that undergraduate computer science majors learn by their third semester, I could forge my address, sending E-mail to the White House or to Newt Gingrich that appeared to be coming from somewhere else.

For instance, I could E-mail a death threat to the president. (Don't do it! This is not a joke.) It has been done. Some people are in a lot of trouble.

A college student in Illinois, for instance, is alleged to have sent a message to President Clinton from a purely fictitious address (Almighty@Never.Gonna.Catch.Me), and the message said, "I am curious, Bill, how would you feel about being the first president to be killed on the same day as his wife?"

Unpleasant stuff, and a federal offense. Despite the attempt at anonymity, the Secret Service tracked the young man down; the kid was caught, charged, and is reported to have confessed.

In Lufkin, Texas, another student is alleged to have pulled a similar prank, trying in this case, however, to make it seem as if the death threat came from his former roommate at Stephen F. Austin State University. He was arrested, too. Presumably, he has a new roommate now. At least for the next five to ten years.

These guys were apprehended, but each and every day people get more and more clever at forging false return addresses, and there is seemingly no end to the resourcefulness of computer hackers, especially the really slimy ones.

Then there is electronic mail going the other way. A clever hacker could potentially, and probably without breaking a very big sweat, send messages to certain people that would appear to be from Bill Clinton. "Please come back to Washington right away, Senator Helms. The president would like to give you a free midnight tour of the Secret Service shooting range," or, "Yes, Mr. Citizen, I happen to agree wholeheartedly with your views on twenty-four-hour term limits, and hereby pledge to devote my full resources to making that goal an immediate reality."

The opportunities for abuse are staggering. Yes, you can pull these pranks by phone or conventional mail, too, but the Internet is new and fancy, so people are presently more prone to play with it. The government hasn't yet figured out convenient routines for dealing with it, either.

Chris Casey at Senator Kennedy's office worries about another potential problem—electronic mailbox stuffing.

"It is very common for interest groups and organizations to use mass mailing campaigns of postcards, letters, telegrams, and so on in order to try to send a message to a member of Congress by inundating them with mail," Casey noted. "Using E-mail, that won't take any organized campaigns, just an individual who feels it is somehow better to send a duplicate electronic message over and over and over again. Unlike postcards stacking up in our mailroom, these messages are bytes, becoming kilobytes and megabytes on that member's computer network!"

In other words, the gun lobby would no longer need volunteers with writer's cramp in order to stuff a mailbox, they could just program a computer, as was done in the case of Crosspost & Spam. The machine could send thousands of messages an hour, all of them perhaps randomized to seem as if they are coming from thousands of different electronic addresses. All it takes is some cleverness and a plug.

Casey explained how, in this instance, the auto-responder offers a hidden benefit. "The unexpected (but effective) side effect of the auto-responder approach is that it discourages such mass mailings by giving back as good as we get."

Send five thousand messages to Senator Kennedy, you see, and you will get five thousand in return. See whose computer blows up first.

If the true wonder of Internet access to government is not the people you can reach, perhaps it is the information that can be uncovered. Most access providers permit you to use a feature called the Internet Gopher, a research tool that burrows rodent-like through countless worldwide computer files in search of the document you need.

The tireless Gopher can even tunnel under the earth, to our nation's capital, below the Office of Management and Budget, under Alice Rivlin's desk, through the thick nap of her royal blue carpet, and retrieve for you the actual Budget of the United States.

You can get it, sure, but the problem is, you then have to read it. Good luck.

And Newt Gingrich himself, shortly after his ascension to

Speaker of the House, announced the opening of a new on-line site called THOMAS (as in Jefferson) where the full text of every House bill since 1992 would be available for public scrutiny. He threatened to also put the Congressional Record on-line, so we could pour over transcripts of each and every speech made on the House floor.

Further on, if you know where to look, you can even uncover the following government offerings:

- Catalog of Federal Domestic Assistance: information about more than one thousand U.S. government assistance programs. (The main reason the Budget is so big.)

- Congressional Office of Technology Assessment Reports: full text of reports produced by the Office of Technology Assessment, which conducts detailed studies for Congress on a wide range of subjects, from climate change to health care reform. (The other reason the Budget is so big.)

- Agricultural Genome Gopher: genome information from the National Agricultural Library system about agriculturally important plants and animals. (No comment.)

- Gazetteer of Planetary Nomenclature: database of planetary place names that have been approved by the International Astronomical Union; courtesy of the U.S. Geological Survey system. (Fascinating.)

- Ribosomal Database Project: access to a database of ribosomal RNA sequences, software useful in manipulating the data, and more. (This, I gotta have!)

Only a tiny sample of course, but frankly, I couldn't even bear to look at the rest. Perhaps I'm simply not enough of a concerned citizen, but access to information like this makes me want to go back into Usenet and search for pictures of swimsuit supermodels. Cindy Crawford has a certain *je ne sais quoi* that I do not find in, for instance, the Speaker of the House.

Back to Thoreau a moment.

Way back when men were men, ponds supported aquatic life, and the federal government had barely enough employees to field a decent softball team, he wrote this:

> But to speak practically and as a citizen, unlike those who call themselves no-government men, I ask for, not at once no government, but *at once* a better government. Let every man make known what kind of government would command his respect, and that will be one step toward obtaining it.

Okay, then—here is the kind of government that would command *my* respect:

- A government where the House sources all have names, and they are allowed to use them.

- A government that either doesn't accept my E-mail or, if it does, has the good sense to answer in kind.

- A government where no men are named for salamanders.

- And, finally, a government where the civil servants keep fully informed, pouring over the Gazetteer of Planetary

Nomenclature, memorizing and cataloging the genomes of every single agriculturally important plant and animal, and keeping fully abreast of the entire Ribosomal Database Project, so that you and I never, ever, ever have to give these important documents a moment's thought.

Isn't that why we pay our civil servants so much money?

chapter ten

THE INCREDIBLE SHRINKING GLOBE

Dissidents on the Net

At 8:19 P.M., Terry Griffith waves both arms like a man struggling to be seen across a crowded train station. He is begging the bartender to kill the sound on the Getaway Café's color television, but when the young man finally sees Terry and heeds his request, a handful of beer drinkers let out a chorus of loud groans. The fifth game of the Stanley Cup finals has just begun, and the Rangers are expected to clinch.

Terry ignores the hockey fans. He picks up his Martin D-35 acoustic guitar, adjusts the strap on his shoulder, and with his whiskey-thick Irish voice starts in at once with the night's first plaintive ballad:

Oh, then tell me Sean O'Farrell, tell me why you hurry so.
Hush, me buchaill, hush and listen
And his cheeks were all a-glow.
I bear orders from the Captain, get ye ready quick and soon
For the pikes must be together by the risin' of the Moon.

The Getaway Café, in suburban Pittsburgh, is all polished brass and wood, a contemporary pub with electronic darts, video trivia, pastel mints at the cash register. The menu is truly multicultural—Italian, Tex-Mex, seafood, and steaks. I am at a corner booth, munching one of those salads that includes not only lettuce and tomato, but grilled chicken, shredded cheese, and french fries, all dumped on top. It is a salad, sure, but about as healthy as deep-fried pork.

Thursday is Irish Night at the Getaway, so the bar is offering a $2.50 special on Guinness drafts. I munch my french-fry salad and watch the Irish music fans drift in, all of them laughing, joking, trading wide smiles. The guys at the bar, though, just stare mournfully at the muted television.

Maybe forty people are in the room by the time Terry finishes his first song. "You're a small crowd," he teases, "but mighty. A mighty small crowd." A few patrons laugh at an old joke, the door flies open, and more of Terry's fans pour in.

Terry is forty-six. He sports a tweed cap, jeans, and a cotton workshirt. His hair is long, back in a ponytail, and peppered with gray; he is small, with wire-rimmed glasses and an open, amicable face.

"The Rising of the Moon" is an Irish traditional, what's known as a rebel song. The "pikes" referred to in the lyric are long poles, hooked at one end, useful around a farm or logging operation, but also commonly used by poor Irish folk for fighting off foreign intruders. In the case of the song, the intruder is no doubt British.

Terry performs a good number of songs about the British presence on Irish soil, because he believes British rule of Northern Ireland is altogether unjust. A few nights each and every week, he uses his guitar to spread the word.

On just about every other day, he uses his modem.

• • •

Griffith is part of yet another Internet culture—that of the international on-line freedom fighters. Access to instantaneous communication such as E-mail, electronic mailing lists, and the trading of files by modem is being used to spread "the message" by thousands of oppressed, misunderstood, angry, wronged, struggling, or simply eager-to-be-heard nationalities across the planet. In nations where war or censorship make free speech a near impossibility, the impact might someday be tremendous.

During the attempted coup against Soviet president Mikhail Gorbachev in 1991, a group of Moscow hackers kept the world (or those who knew where to look, at least) completely up to date. At the height of the Bosnian civil war, a man named Wam Kat in Zagreb, Croatia, used the Net much like the French underground once used the telegraph, letting the outside world know the inside scoop. Chinese leaders, though they've recently agreed to do business with Microsoft Corporation, are reported to be afraid of the Net for the same reason they have outlawed satellite dishes: an informed populace can be a dangerous one. And Vietnam is getting a CompuServe connection.

It is not just the United States government that worries about the Net. By early 1995 nearly 160 countries were reachable by E-mail, and some Internet supporters see this as the final breakdown of state boundaries, a first step in the fulfillment of the New Age "one planet, one people" revolution. If we all understand one another, the argument goes, if we can communicate regularly and during crises, there will be no war. It will become increasingly hard for ruthless rulers to characterize the "enemy" as a horned infidel if the citizenry and the "enemy" have spent months trading gardening tips. "But he helped me save my roses!" will be the rallying cry of the twenty-first century.

Like every other claim made about the Internet, of course, the claim of international serenity might be a tad optimistic, but I concede that the possibilities are very interesting.

"As more and more people have access to the Internet," Siobhan Down, program director for the international writers' group PEN, predicted in *The New York Times*, "it will be practically impossible to ban something." Already, activists are throwing banned books up on the Net—the works of Chinese dissident Wei Jingsheng, Indonesian novelist Pramoedya Ananta Toer and Iranian writer Esmail Fassih. The books are stored on a computer in Hackensack, New Jersey, of all places, and can be accessed via an address on the Internet.

It is more feasible for an oppressive government to listen into a phone call or intercept a fax, experts say, than it is for them to intercept or trace E-mail. The reason has to do with how Internet data is broken up and sent. Like Wam Kat before them, a lone dissident with a modem in Beijing or Tehran, Belfast or Grozny, could conceivably tap into zillions of gigabytes of outside information, then turn around and broadcast the inside story of his oppression across the globe.

This access is not always so easy, however. There are very few Radio Shacks in the Third World.

For instance, Jeff Cochrane, a researcher in Ghana, Africa, preparing to work under a Fulbright scholarship in Sierra Leone, responded to my request for information on his Internet hookup with the following note:

Fri, 3 Jun 1994 19:01:01-0400

Received your note yesterday via a Fidonet
dial-up download from my hotel room in Accra,
which involved taking off the cover of my room
phone, attaching alligator clips to the incoming wires of the phone at one end and to my
modem jack at the other, then dialing reception
to have them call USA Direct, then telling ATT
to dial a Fidonet server in Washington DC and
bill it to my credit card, then quickly drop-
ping the mouthpiece of my phone out so that
room noise would not interfere with the data
transmission, watching as my outgoing mail was
uploaded and then my incoming mail was down-
loaded, then disconnecting everything and re-
assembling my phone. At least in Ghana there's
reliable power to keep my computer battery
charged, and when you pick up the phone re-
ceiver there's almost always a dial tone. In
Sierra Leone, this will not be the case.

It is not as easy as dialing up America Online and pointing
your mouse at a little box that says "Overthrow the Regime." But
obviously, connecting to the Net can be done—all over the
world.

There are an enormous number of international groups on
the Internet, but most of them are not revolutionary in the least.
On Usenet for instance, there are groups for almost every eth-

nic cluster, from soc.culture.african to soc.culture.yugoslavia, with soc.culture.berber, soc.culture.nigeria, and soc.culture.tamil somewhere in the middle. All in all, when I last counted, there were sixty-eight of these groups, with more being added every day.

If you are trying to find an argument, this is the place to look for one. In fact, just mention Turkey or Armenia in just about any group, and the argument will find you.

Still, much of what concerns those who post on the international newsgroups mirrors what concerns us all. Soc.culture.indian, for instance, is not only one of the most popular soc.culture groups, but published usage statistics show it is one of the most highly used newsgroups on all of Usenet. When you call soc.culture.indian up on your screen, the menu will be fat with messages, and the list of topics will look something like this:

```
Anybody Going from Detroit to Madras?
Arranged Marriages
Cheap Ticket from JFK to India
Goan Arts and Crafts
Goat meat
Hindu Apologists!
Hindu Holidays
Hindu Shame? Gimme a break!
Looking for an Indian female
Looking for a Hindu-Punjabi Girl
Suspect Names Pakistan in Bombings
Time to get a Visa
```

Which is, perhaps, the point. Except for a few dietary differences, and different names we use for God, the peoples of the

world are not all that different. We like a bargain; we are looking for love.

Terry Griffith's concerns, however, are Irish. When he isn't per-
forming his rendition of "They Wounded Old Ireland," he is using
his computer to scan newsgroups such as soc.culture.celtic,
picking up information on the continuing British presence in
Northern Ireland, and downloading copies of *The Irish Emigrant,* a weekly recap of news from the Emerald Isle. The *Emigrant* is edited by Liam Ferrie of Galway, and his story itself is a
model of how the Internet can unexpectedly transform people's
lives. Ferrie worked in Galway for Digital Equipment Corporation in 1987 when he started his electronic newsletter as a service
to twenty or so fellow employees—colleagues who had transferred overseas and might miss the local news. The newsletter was
distributed by what is known as a listserver (an automated mailing list that sends electronic mail instead of Lands' End catalogs.)

"The distribution list started to grow immediately," Ferrie
explained to me by E-mail, "as I heard of additional Irish nation-
als working for Digital, and they heard about me." His mailing
list grew rapidly to include five hundred Digital employees, from
Hong Kong to Czechoslovakia, and some of his colleagues began
distributing the newsletter to people outside of Digital, until the
distribution list approached four thousand. Then Digital closed
its Galway plant.

"I was faced with the choice of leaving Galway to find work or
to turn the *Emigrant* into a commercial enterprise," Ferrie wrote.
"Galway is a place which most people find difficult to leave, and

I was no exception." He started to charge a small fee for E-mail subscriptions to his newsletter. The response has been strong, and the electronic newspaper is now Ferrie's full-time occupation. He even has a subscriber at the Amundsen-Scott base at the South Pole.

Terry Griffith subscribes, then takes his copy of the *Emigrant,* prints it out on a laser printer, makes a handful of photocopies, and leaves them on the cigarette machine at Murphy's Pour House, an Irish pub south of Pittsburgh. Murphy's is frequented by both Irish-Americans and a handful of Irish students studying or working in the states, and over time, Griffith has learned to print the *Emigrant* in a large, bold font, so that it can be read in a dark, smoky room.

"I've seen some of the students at Murphy's read the *Emigrant* and get an astonished look on their faces," Griffith tells me between sets. "A couple months ago this guy was reading and he says, 'Oh-my-God.' I say, 'What's the matter?' He was reading the obituaries, and he says, 'I knew that fella.' Of course, a lot of them will turn right to the back, to the sports scores."

This is not exactly James Bond stuff—the results of Saturday's match between the Balbriggan Ballknockers and the Skibbereen Skidoos is not so dramatic as what happened in the former Soviet Union, or in Bosnia-Herzegovina—but in his own small way, by helping to distribute Ferrie's paper in the United States, Griffith sees himself as engaged in a subversive act.

Much of the English language news coming out of the British Isles is written by reporters based in London, he explains, and "the conventional news is cleared through [a division of British intelligence known as] MI5 before it goes out over the wire."

Griffith smiles, raises an eyebrow. "And they have been known to distort."

While the *Emigrant* regularly chronicles Northern Irish violence and politics, it comes out of the Republic of Ireland and bypasses normal news distribution channels by coming across the Net. In this way, Griffith says, Ferrie's paper also bypasses British oversight. "During World War II, the Allies would never have relied on news coming out of a German News Agency," he explains. "Why wouldn't someone question news about Ireland that has come from or through Great Britain's censors?"

All of this was before the 1994 ceasefire between the British government and the Irish Republican army, by the way. In the pre-peace days, for instance, Gerry Adams, leader of Sinn Fein, the IRA's political wing, was not even allowed to appear on British television without an actor dubbing in his voice. (In other words, British viewers could hear his words, they just couldn't hear *him* say them. Odd rule.) Now, Adams is all over British television and is even allowed to travel into London.

There is no direct connection, of course, maybe no connection at all, but to the extent that public opinion and pressure from the American government played a part in coercing the British and Sinn Fein leaders to settle their conflict, it is entirely possible that Griffith and Liam Ferrie played their small part in bringing a moment of peace to Northern Ireland.

What can foreign governments do about this newly found freedom of information?

Well, again, censoring the Net is a problem, because no one

person or one group "publishes" or "broadcasts" the Net. There is no center, no headquarters, no home office. The Net is thousands of smaller networks all linked together, traversing national and continental boundaries. So who do you censor?

Nor can it be easily shut down. To disconnect all access to the Internet, to keep his citizenry from writing messages to the international Net community or reading messages from them, a tyrant would theoretically have to confiscate every computer within his borders, or shut down the entire phone system. Otherwise, anyone with a computer and phone line could log on, and the government would be hard-pressed to know about it. Confiscating computers or shutting down a national phone network would probably work, but it is not the cleverest way to win public support, especially in a world economy.

Still, censorship has been attempted.

Take Italy for instance, where machine-gun-toting police raided the offices of 119 local bulletin board systems in May 1994, confiscating computer hardware, disks, and answering machines. Police were trying to crack down on a ring of software pirates (who copy software illegally, to avoid paying for it, and sell it to others without paying licensing fees) said to be run by two men in Pesaro. The two men were suspected of distributing the software through bulletin boards, so the Italian police shut all 119 of them down. Classic overkill, many charged. The police couldn't find the well-hidden pirates, so they went after the easily located bulletin board operators, though the operators were arguably blameless for the abuses of two users.

Or consider the response of another highly repressive dictatorship: Canada!

In early 1994, a Canadian judge ordered a publication ban on facts relating to the gruesome murders of two teenage girls. The Teale-Homolka case was deemed so sensational, the manner of death so lurid, that any pretrial publicity, including reports of the apparent confession of one of those charged, was totally outlawed by the judge. Canadian newspapers could not carry a word. Copies of neighboring American newspapers—*The Buffalo News* and the *Detroit News,* for instance—did carry the story but were confiscated at the border.

Two students, however—Justin Wells at the University of Waterloo and Ken Chasse at the University of Toronto—noticed that the publication ban had become a hot topic on a newsgroup called ont.general ("ont," as in Ontario). Wells and Chasse created their own newsgroup, alt.fan.karla-homolka, as a "sick joke," using the name of one of the alleged murderers. Canadians and others quickly took to the group, however, to trade banned information and post newspaper articles from the American press. When Canadian universities, fearing they would get in trouble, deleted the alt.fan.karla-homolka group from their students' accounts, two new groups were formed, and the numbers of postings only grew. One whimsical Canadian suggested that all banned Teale-Homolka news should be posted to rec.sport.hockey, since no Canadian government official would ever dream of shutting that one down.

The Ontario attorney general's office eventually got into the act, investigating one frequent poster known as Lt. Starbuck and warning others that their computers could be seized if violations continued. Some users claim that private E-mail messages were electronically scanned for any reference to the Teale-Homolka case. Lots and lots of Canadians are still angry about this whole affair—the judge and the police, because in the end the ban was made useless, and the Internet zealots, because no one messes with their Net.

Back at the Getaway, Terry confesses that, though he is clearly of good Irish stock, he is not so sure who came over on what boat, or when. "I knew my relatives were Irish," he tells me, "but they wouldn't talk about it. That's always a sign that there is something shaky going on.

"My grandfather died when I was five," he continues. "He wasn't born in Ireland—his father was born in Ireland, but he just maintained his Irishness and sang a lot of songs. I always open with 'The Rising of the Moon,' because it's a song I can remember him singing."

Griffith started playing Irish music in the sixties, "when Peter, Paul and Mary and the Kingston Trio and everyone was doing it," but he found there was no money. "Then about ten years ago it became a good thing to put in bars. It draws a certain audience that knows how to drink, which is a good thing for a bar to do." Indeed.

At the Getaway, the Guinness draft flows like the River Shannon after a storm, the occasional shot of Jameson whiskey is hoisted high to salute Sinn Fein, and the crowd, which has swelled to nearly eighty people over the course of the long evening, grows louder and more appreciative of the rebel tunes. Even Terry's good friend Shag, though, can't help but rest one eye on the television. The New York Rangers hold a lead, and it looks as if the series will wrap itself up.

"If you had told me a few years ago that I, through my computer, would be providing information to the local Irish community that they couldn't get any other way, I would have told you that you were nuts," Terry admits, "but that's exactly what I'm doing."

And exactly what thousands of others are doing as well. Modems beep and whine across the planet. Data streams cross the globe in fractions of seconds. Canadians get censored news with their hockey. And somewhere in Sierra Leone, Jeff Cochrane is trying to find a working phone booth so he can unscrew the phone's mouthpiece, latch on his alligator clips, and send E-mail home. The world may or may not become a better place thanks to the Internet, but it seems to have become a much smaller place. And to the man in Dublin who sent me the recipes for curried chicken, a belated thanks.

chapter eleven

THE NIGHT THOREAU HAD CYBERSEX

Or, Once You're On, How Do You Get Off?

Late one evening, as I was nearing the end of my one-year journey into the Internet's deep, uncharted electronic woods, Thoreau came to me in a dream. He had dark, tousled hair and one of those beards that rings the bottom of the jaw, and his mouth was drawn into a scowl. He looked surprisingly like Abe Lincoln, only shorter.

"We are conscious of an animal in us," he said out of nowhere, his voice soft and deep. "It is reptile and sensual, and perhaps cannot be wholly expelled."

"What?" I asked.

"An animal in us," he repeated. "Reptile and sensual."

It was only then I noticed that Thoreau was carrying a dead otter, tethered on a rope. The otter was wet, and there was an unpleasant smell. "I don't know what you're asking me," I said.

"What is chastity?" Thoreau grunted back. "How shall a man know if he is chaste?"

"I don't know," I insisted, "but that otter has to go."

• • •

It was only a dream, of course, but he had a good point. Here I was, close to finishing this book, with only the barest mention of sex and the Net. Why?

I'm basically a shy person, easily embarrassed. My idea of a good, long discussion about sex is saying, "I want to, do you want to?" Yet it seems like most everyone else on the planet would rather discuss sex than any other topic available. People talk about sex on television. People pay to talk about sex with strangers on the telephone. Senators from Utah talk about sex at hearings of the Judiciary Committee. People cannot get enough, it seems, so why should the Information Superhighway be any different?

Well, it isn't.

Net users have devised countless ways to talk about sex, and even a few ways to have sex (assuming actual bodily contact is not a high priority). The proliferation of sex discussion groups on the Net has been a source of amusement for some and outrage for others, but none of this has slowed it down. At last count, there were 42 separate sex discussion groups within Usenet, including such oddities as:

```
alt.sex
alt.sex.bestiality
alt.sex.bestiality.barney
alt.sex.bondage
alt.sex.breast
alt.sex.fetish.feet
alt.sex.fetish.hair
alt.sex.fetish.startrek
alt.sex.magazines
```

```
alt.sex.movies
alt.sex.spanking
alt.sex.woody-allen
```

And I have left out the ones that I'm too embarrassed to even mention. For instance, alt.sex.fetish.diapers, which I hope is someone's idea of a joke, and alt.sex.fetish.watersports, which has nothing at all to do with swim meets. Frankly, I'm having trouble even thinking of a topic that *isn't* covered.

The alt.sex assortment is not only one of the raciest neighborhoods on the Net, it is also one of the most popular. Computer wizards with fancy software and lots of free time compile statistics on how many people send messages to a particular newsgroup and how many people read those messages. Near the top of the monthly Top 40, consistently, are alt.sex, alt.sex.stories, alt.sex.bondage, rec.arts.movies, and misc.jobs.offered.

This seems, perhaps, to be a fairly representative illustration of what people want to do with their lives: talk about sex, go to the movies, and if there is any time left over, find a good-paying job.

Thoreau returned the next night, and the night after that. In some of the dreams, he had a fishing pole and a lopsided grin; in others he was holding a quill pen to his temple, looking quite the studious author. His jacket was always black, but needed a good dry cleaning. He wanted to know more than I could tell him.

"I fear," he rumbled, "that we are such gods or demigods only as fawns and satyrs, the divine allied to beasts, the creatures of appetite, and that, to some extent, our very life is our disgrace."

"What?" I asked again.

He shook his head, as if I had disappointed him. "I would fain know," he repeated, "how shall a man know if he is chaste?"

The easiest way to shame a writer is to accuse him of insufficient research, and Thoreau was writer enough to know that. His words did not make total sense to me, but I think he was suggesting I had ducked the issue, that I had not probed deeply enough. I had no choice but to meet his challenge.

So I went, notebook at my side, read the main sex group thoroughly, recorded my field observations, and here is what I found: Alt.sex is fairly docile. A typical evening's sample of subjects might include condom use, various methods of female birth control, breast size preference, the importance of male magnitude, the perpetual "What Do Women Really Want?" query, and assorted helpful little tips to improve one's performance, duration, or accuracy.

For instance, one nervous novice posted a question to alt.sex about basic boudoir technique. How, he wondered, if the situation should ever present itself, would he know if he was doing it right? He specifically wanted to "make her go crazy."

A presumably more experienced practitioner responded with this advice, "There is no one way to do it, so instructions wouldn't help. The main thing to keep in mind is simply how she reacts to what you do. Listen for changes in her breathing, or the sudden contraction of muscles."

Notwithstanding the fact that this advice applies just as well to cardiopulmonary resuscitation as lovemaking, I thought the guy did a pretty good job of explaining a fairly complicated subject in simple, basic terms. He might, in fact, do very well in a technical writing class. Most everyone else responded with fanciful boasts about how *they* did it, and how deliciously insane they managed to drive their sex partner. I believed none of them.

People post fiction to the group as well, but most of the stories seem to be little more than the endlessly banal fantasies of desperate young men (more men than women post here)—the types of "true" stories that get published in *Penthouse* Forum: "I was hot, I was ready, and my landlady didn't seem to mind."

A few—very few—alt.sex posters have read their Anaïs Nin, however, and try, at least, for metaphor. Let me quote from one, in which the female has been mysteriously transformed into a white horse:

"He looked about for a saddle. There was none. He heard a soft, feminine voice whisper, 'Ride me. Ride me till morning.' He became suddenly aware of an erection. He cleared his throat."

It was about that time I cleared my screen.

"My gratitude for that," Thoreau said on his next visit. He looked long and hard at my bedroom curtains, picked at his teeth with a twig he had carried into my dream, then turned in my direction and smiled. "The generative energy invigorates and inspires us."

"What?"

He smiled again, nodded cheerfully, insistently. He clearly wanted to know more.

To be honest, I started to suspect old Thoreau of something beyond simple intellectual curiosity here, but that is just conjecture. I do know that he spent an awful lot of time alone in that cabin.

In any case, I tried to locate some less-traveled corner of the woods for him, something to further invigorate and inspire him, and I found that it was but a short walk from alt.sex to alt.sex.fetish.feet.

Oddly, or at least to my naïve surprise, the alt.sex.fetish.feet people seemed more serious than the plain old alt.sex people. The amateurs had been left behind, perhaps. There was an immediately apparent urgency to the postings on alt.sex.fetish.feet. Topics on the night I visited included a foot fetish quiz and discussions of leather shoes; of high heels; of toenails (painted and unpainted); of leg fetishes, shoe catalogs, voyeurism, and "celebrity feet."

The hot question while I was reading this male-dominated group was voiced thusly, "If a man has dorky feet, we can still develop a business or social relationship. With a woman on the other hand, I might have a business or semisocial relationship, but it is doubtful a sensual attraction would develop. I wonder if this fetish of ours is replicated in the female species?"

The messages that followed seemed to share the original poster's sentiments, but no women came forward to offer their opinion, so the question was ultimately unresolved.

Then there is bondage.

I was raised Catholic, attended Catholic school for twelve interminable years. My educational background perhaps explains my discomfort with all aspects of sex talk, and many aspects of sex, and given this, the mere idea of a sadomasochistic or bondage relationship is extremely difficult for me to fathom. At this stage of my life, bondage is just not a personal priority. When I go shopping, I shop for pants that fit more loosely around the waist, not ones that bind. The only thing tying me down right now is too much work and my daughter's kindergarten schedule. If I wish to be lightly flogged, I have an editor.

But alt.sex.bondage is certainly impressive. These people are immeasurably brave. I wouldn't even think some of this stuff, much less type it onto a computer screen and send it to a worldwide newsgroup where potentially thousands might read it and figure out who I am. Nicknames are the norm here, but accounts can sometimes be traced.

Topics on alt.sex.bondage range from the technical, as in "Cleaning procedures for whips," to shopping queries such as "Looking for locking buckles," to information on bondage clubs and private parties, and on to people's own stories of S&M encounters, real and imagined.

In a message titled "Essences of Spanking," a person who did not reveal his or her gender wrote about the proper use of a frame and block. "I kneel naked on the bench and place my hands and head in a stock at the front of the frame. My body is hinged over the rear block and my waist is strapped down. Then my legs are spread and strapped. This forces me to arch my back and stick my bottom out in the air." The message goes on awhile to describe the actual spanking, with a British cane. The description is offered in all seriousness.

Another writer, again with no hint of irony or wit, posted a message titled "50 Ways to Tie Your Lover." He listed all fifty, in cold detail, with no further comment. "Arms crossed behind," one read, "wrists bound to each other by a tether." Oddly enough, that was how Thoreau had tied the otter, the one he carried into my room that first night.

But when I came across a long, thoughtful discussion on gagging, and the suggestion that a golf ball with eye screws in opposite sides and a raw-hide strap might work well as a muzzle, giving a "durable, and playful texture," I figured it was time for me to go.

By the end of the week, Thoreau was coming into my dreams more and more often, seeming more and more agitated. He shuffled his big boots nervously on my bedroom floor (I would check in the mornings, but there were never any scuff marks or other outward proof). He bit nervously at his nails, all ashenfaced and disheveled, scowled repeatedly but didn't speak.

He just kept blinking his eyes, open and shut, open and shut, as if it were some signal. I could only guess, but I eventually surmised what the man wanted were pictures, something to look at.

And yes, there are pictures on the Net, plenty of them, from the suggestive, to the erotic, to the obscene. The technology to scan photographs into electronic form, transmit them across phone lines, and download them into our homes is fast becoming widespread. On the Net, these pictures are called binaries, referring to the basic logical "on-off" language of computers. (The more usual definition of binary is "something made up of two parts," but the joke here is too obvious.) The other Internet term is GIF, short for Graphic Interchange Format—more of that jargon that keeps technoids from actually making sense. The pictures come across the electronic lace doily as numbers—ones and zeros—and special software is needed to transform them back into recognizable shapes.

Within Usenet, there is alt.binary.pictures.erotica.females, alt.binary.pictures.erotica.male, alt.binaries.pictures.erotica.blondes, and many more. A good number of the photos found on these groups are scanned in illegally from popular skin magazines, and the sophistication of your computer's graphics card and software will determine whether what you see is erotic or just fuzzy.

Many people are truly upset, though, about the very real possibility that an eleven-year-old could conceivably search, find, and stare at these pictures. But I look at it this way—any kid with enough technical savvy to hook up a modem, find an Internet connection, dial in, negotiate the software, download binary files, decode them, and make them appear as intended on the screen, could probably figure out how to come up with five dollars and locate a magazine rack. Sure, kids could potentially find some pretty raw stuff here, but they would find it much faster under their older brother's mattress. Mom and Pop should probably just keep an eye on the computer room.

And there is another sexual outlet on the Net—cybersex, the evil twin of cyberspace. Cybersex is sex without touching, sex without seeing, sex without even hearing the other person's voice. It is sex by typing, and reading, and lots of folks are all hot up about it.

People tried to explain cybersex to me back when I was unacquainted with the term, and I ended up just staring at them blankly. Then, after imagining that perhaps I understood, I tried to explain cybersex to others, and they ended up just staring at me blankly. Cybersex, admittedly, is hard to describe, but get your blank stares ready, because I am going to try.

Cybersex is talking dirty in real time, describing various sexual acts in chronological and intimate detail, with a partner who could be anything or anyone you could possibly imagine. Here is how it is done:

1. Two people sit alone in front of their respective computers, anywhere in the world.

2. They type onto the screen a description of what they might be doing to one another if they were not separated by three thousand miles, marriage, total lack of acquaintance, and the fact that one of them is really just a thirteen-year-old boy pretending to be a voluptuous blonde woman of twenty-five.

3. When they type these descriptions, such as "I am ripping off your blouse in a passionate frenzy," the description is read almost immediately by the other person and that person types a response. "Careful, it's faux silk."

4. They sometimes do things in the privacy of their own homes that would embarrass me, but maybe not Jocelyn Elders.

I just reread that step-by-step description, and now *I* have that blank stare again.

Let me try to clear this up by example.

I noticed that a woman named Martha was posting to the alt.sex group frequently, often discussing the positive aspects of her cybersexual interludes. I sent Martha an electronic mail message and asked her to tell me what she found so attractive about computer sex.

"Some may consider it adultery," she wrote back. "Others, like me, see it as a means of release, and pure innocent sexual gratification, for both involved. In fact, if anything, it *stops* me from having an affair in the physical sense."

Martha is a twenty-nine-year-old graphic artist from Chicago, and she is married. I asked her to explain how a cybersex relationship develops.

"Although Cybersex allows one to have 'sex' with whomever they please," she told me, "I've found that I can't just 'jump' into sex with just anyone. That's too unfeeling, and not at all satisfying. How can I imagine the person if I don't know anything about him? I have to develop a mental image of him, by knowing what his general appearance is . . . hair, eye color, height, build . . . just a general portrait. Then, through hours of conversation, I allow my instincts to take over."

She explained that her "most satisfying scenario" is corresponding with someone for weeks or months before anything happens. She met one fellow that way, began to chat quite casually, and eventually felt a strong attraction. "Night after night we'd talk—learning everything there was to know about each other. Every secret, every thought, every detail was revealed.

We'd tell each other things that we could barely tell ourselves, let alone anyone else!"

Then, despite embarrassment and reservations, they tried it. They joked around, pretending to be having sex in a burning house, or during a cyclone. But eventually, she wrote, "our crazy sex began to calm down. It began to grow more sensuous, more tender, more *real*. Each occasion, we became closer and closer, and when it was over, we'd hold each other in our arms, whispering and touching each other softly. These became magical moments for us both."

Understand, they've never met.

She even sent me a transcript of a cybersex encounter, but first—*first*, so relax for a moment—I have to explain yet another technical marvel—Internet Relay Chat, or IRC, or just Chat. Usenet postings and E-mail both have certain time lags. While the mail or bulletin board message you type and send may reach its destination in seconds or minutes, it will usually then sit there for anywhere from hours to days to weeks before it is read. Usenet messages are stored on a machine somewhere until you and I retrieve the message. Electronic mail sits on the hard disk of your access provider in what is known as an E-mail queue, until you decide to read your E-mail.

But Chat messages don't sit anywhere. When you log into a Chat system (and how you do it differs widely, depending on software and who you have chosen for an access provider, so I will spare you the technical details), you type in a certain command to join a "channel." Every IRC channel has a name, like "chatzone," or "wasteland," or "hottub," and depending on the channel and the time of day, there might be ten or twenty other people hooked in. When you type, "Hello, how are you wild and crazy guys?" onto your screen, that message appears on the screens of the ten or twenty others on the channel almost at once, whether they are three blocks away or in Oulu, Finland. If the guy in Finland, a guy named Heikki, types back, "I'm just fine, thanks," that will appear on everyone's screen as well. Of course, if Heikki were that polite, he wouldn't be on IRC.

There are two sides to the IRC. To its credit, the relay chat system was used to dramatic effect during the 1993 coup attempt against Russian president Boris Yeltsin, keeping the world instantaneously updated on troop movements and Stolichnaya shipments. To its discredit, IRC is used much of the rest of the time by college students, geeks, weirdos, and bores who have nothing to say and can't stop saying it.

But IRC is where cybersex happens, because cybersex needs to be spontaneous and instantaneous, not remote and sporadic. Cybersex happens on IRC because when a man rips away a woman's faux silk blouse, he wants her to know it, and he wants her to know it right away.

So, without further ado, here is the transcript Martha sent me of her cybersexual interlude with Guy (name changed). It is none of our business really, but here it is:

```
<Guy> okay—light the fire
<Martha> throwing kindling on newspapers
  . . . striking match . . . Poof! Blaze.
<Guy> You're wearing a sheer negligee—a present
  from your hubby which you've saved to two-time
  him.
<Martha> Of course . . . he's never seen me in
  it. . . .
<Guy> it's a teddy, with G-string
```

<Martha> Yes, and that string is starting to
rub against me . . . turning me on . . .
<Guy> a long one would catch fire from the fire
lapping at our feet. I'm just wearing a
towel, after a long, hot shower
<Martha> You smell so so good, as I nuzzle your
neck and kiss your ear
<Guy> you put your hands on my shoulders, my
hands go to your hips
<Martha> Looking up at you . . . into your
amazing green eyes, I kiss you . . .
deeply . . .
<Guy> I bring my face around to kiss your neck,
you lift your head & pull it back
<Guy> my hand kneads your hip, playing with the
string
<Martha> fingering my string, I place my hands
on your ass, and pull you into me . . . then
I rip off your towel
<Guy> you press against me, feeling me through
the thick towel
<Martha> No, the towel is gone now . . . but I
feel your rock hard penis against me
<Guy> my hardness is up against you, you press
into it. You bring your hands down to take it all

Martha herself did some editing here before sending the
transcript along to me, explaining that matters had gotten too
graphic. We pick up some moments later:

<Martha> I can feel you begin to slow . . . our
mouths together . . . our sweaty bodies rub-
bing against each other

```
<Guy> I can smell your sweet, musky smell
 between us and breathe it in deeply
<Martha> So can I! and we lay down together,
 still breathing heavily . . . and kiss, and
 look at each other, and giggle! oh how sweet
 you are!!!!!!
<Guy> It's quite an amazing sight
<Guy> we hold each other tenderly, and
 holding each other, drift gently off to
 sleep.
<Martha> You are, without a doubt, the most
 amazing person. You turn me on so much, its
 scary!
<Guy> it's all in the mind, darling
```

Sweet, tender, electronic, unreal. That's cybersex. But Martha swears by it, and she and Guy stay in touch, even though she tells me the affair is over. "Seeing his sweet name on my E-mail list always brings a smile to my face," she writes. "And now, here we are, two lovers, painfully separated by a half of a country, and marriages, kids, lifestyles. The fact that we've never physically met or have never spoken to each other orally is insignificant. We fell in love with our minds, not our physical bodies. But oh, how frustrating it can be! Just to have him hold me for real, to make love to him and his body would probably ruin me for sex for the rest of my life."

She doesn't even know the man's name, just the name he has chosen for Internet correspondence. They will probably never meet, yet it seems obvious she is carrying a big torch for him. For some, at least, cybersex is a tangible thing.

• • •

But Thoreau? Well the old philosopher, it turns out, surely did spend too much time alone in that small cabin, reading Homer, staring out at the ever-frozen pond, contemplating lives of quiet desperation, because the next thing I knew, he was standing over my bed again.

"I care not how obscene my *words* are," he shouted, jumping up and down like a schoolboy. "We discourse freely without shame of one form of sensuality, and are silent about another. From exertion comes wisdom and purity."

It took me a moment to get his meaning, but I eventually did. "You want me to *try* it?" I shouted back. "You want me to actually try this stuff?"

He quieted down, nodded, then gave me a wink. "It is neither the quality nor the quantity, but the devotion to sensual savors," he whispered. "I would fain know."

I awoke at that moment, and of course there was no one there. The dream had gone *poof.* Thoreau was conveniently gone, but not my writerly guilt. He was eager to know, and perhaps my readers would be as well.

So I found my way into Chat and typed the commands to enter a channel called Netsex, which seemed promising enough.

When you log into the IRC system, by the way, the first thing you do is choose a nickname (by typing nick=<whatever>.) I considered the nickname <Henry David> but doubted that would elicit much sensual interest, so I opted instead for the

nickname <Lover>, presuming that would make my intentions
perfectly clear.

What follows is a transcript of my first cybersexual experience, with a woman named <Chris>, and numerous interrup-
tions from a guy named <Bulge>:

```
<Bulge> Is everyone having a cigarette? Where's
  all the sex?
<Chris> How about you?
<Bulge> Nope.
<Chris> Oh well
<Bulge> Is this the sex channel?
<Chris> Yep.
<Bulge> Are you m or f Chris?
<Chris> f
<Bulge> How old?
<Chris> 24
```

I jumped in here, realizing that there was an alleged female
on the channel, and feeling a strong urge to complete my
research. I will explain the alleged part later.

```
<Lover> Can you tell me how to have cybersex?
<Chris> Okay, first go and find a girl . . .
<Bulge> Will a blow up doll do?
<Chris> No a blow up doll is too passive.
<Lover> Can we have cybersex?
<Chris> You don't even know me.
<Lover> I know, but I'm really interested in
  learning how cybersex works.
<Chris> I know how it works. I've done it nine
  or ten times.
```

```
<Lover> How is it done?
<Chris> Have you ever masturbated in front of
  another person?
<Lover> That is too embarrassing to even think
  about answering.
<Chris> Why? Are you fat?
<Lover> No, I play lots of tennis.
<Chris> Then you'd have nothing to be embar-
  rassed about. Or is your penis too small?
<Lover> Are we going to have cybersex, or are
  you just teasing me?
<Chris> Let's start again, but don't rush. Go
  slowly.
<Lover> Okay. I think you are nice.
<Chris> Thank you.
<Lover> I am six foot tall, sandy hair. You?
<Chris> I am 5'10", brown hair, 36C breasts,
  and a cute butt.
<Lover> You sound pretty.
```

But, unfortunately, immediately at the mention of Chris's posterior, something strange happened. A crowd of Chat types whose nicknames were <JoyBoy>, <Lucifer>, <Lonewolf>, and <SpErM> hurriedly joined the channel and began the Chat-channel equivalent of wolf whistling. Perhaps they had been listening in all along; I don't fully understand how they would do that, but I know enough to know that clever computer users can do a lot that the normal user cannot. In any case, <Chris>, understandably put off by such an assembly, began to insist that the only way we could really have sex was if I drove to Cincinnati. The other men started to harass her, saying they wanted sex, too, and demanding information on other parts of her anatomy.

Seconds later, this message showed up at the bottom of my screen:

```
*** <Chris> parts channel #Netsex
```

She was gone, and who could blame her?

Sad, really. Perhaps <Chris> was a woman with whom I might have found happiness. Perhaps we were destined for one another's arms. Perhaps we might have had something very, very special.

Or perhaps she was a guy.

For all I know, <Chris> may have been <Bulge> logging in somehow under twin nicknames. <Chris> might have been anything, or anyone, but chances are she was not actually a woman. You see, there is a well-documented dearth of females on IRC, for two reasons. One is that there are still more male computer whizbangs in the world than there are female computer whizbangs, though that is changing. The second reason is that any woman who does show up to Chat is immediately surrounded by a large crowd of men asking her rude and insensitive questions. Women tend to have two intelligent reactions to this onslaught of unwanted notice: they leave, or they adopt a new nickname like <Bruiser> and never tell a soul.

In response to this, countless men have pretended to be women on IRC, just as some of them do in the other areas of the Internet. There is often no way to tell, and it is an excellent way to get attention.

My first attempt at cybersex frustrated, Thoreau's words still ringing in my ears, I had no alternative it seemed but to gender-switch myself. Heck, they do it in Shakespeare's plays all the time. It is almost a literary tradition.

Since a clever computer navigator could probably find out my university account number, and thus my initials, I chose <Deb> as my new nickname. Soon after that, my Deb persona wandered onto the Netsex channel of IRC, just to see what was happening.

I felt almost immediately like a bright light in a field of mosquitoes. I could hardly keep up with the high number of greetings blinking on my monochrome monitor. I had countless suitors within minutes, but I chose a fellow nicknamed <By-Tor> to be my sex partner. He came on to me like a barrel of beer-drunk monkeys, and gosh, he sounded kinda cute.

He even persuaded me to leave the Netsex channel and, through the wizardry of IRC, created a whole new channel on which we could meet in privacy. He called it Lovechild.

Here, then, is our complete encounter, in all its ludicrous glory:

```
<By-tor> undresses Deb
<Deb> My button is stuck
<By-tor> pulls button off
<Deb> Ping!
<By-tor> pulls deb's dress? blouse? off
<Deb> Okeedokee
<By-tor> What are you wearing now?
<Deb> Just my jeans
<By-tor> unzippers your jeans with his teeth
```

\<Deb\> Yikes
\<By-tor\> caresses your supple breasts
\<Deb\> With what?
\<By-tor\> notices the erect nipples
\<Deb\> Good observation skills
\<By-tor\> licks in circles around the erect
 nipples
\<Deb\> Don't make yourself dizzy!
\<By-tor\> grabs the massage oil and turns down
 the lights
\<Deb\> Yikes. I can't see. That oil is hot.
\<By-tor\> thinks you'll grow to like it. He puts
 on soft music.
\<Deb\> Is that Barry Manilow I hear?
\<By-tor\> Yes, Barry baby.
\<Deb\> By-tor you big, wild boy you.
\<By-tor\> whispers sweet nothings in your ear
\<Deb\> Like what, for instance?
\<By-tor\> pops open the best bottle of champagne
\<Deb\> Can't drink. Allergies.
\<By-tor\> The champagne is for me then
\<Deb\> Are you just telling me these things to
 get sex?
\<By-tor\> would never do that
\<Deb\> I'm totally naked and running around the
 room screaming.
\<By-tor\> notices your heavy breathing
\<Deb\> I think I'm freaking out
\<By-tor\> grabs you and licks your hot spot
\<Deb\> My parents are home! My parents are home!
\<By-tor\> No they aren't

```
<Deb> They're coming up the stairs. Hide, By-tor,
  under the bed.
<By-tor> hides under the bed
<Deb> Hi, Ma!
<By-tor> is scared
<Deb> No, Ma, no one was here. That was the radio.
```

At this point, by typing the chat command "nick=<Ma>," I instantaneously switch my nickname to <Ma>. <By-tor> remains huddled under the bed, understandably confused.

```
<Ma> You little whore! Slap!
```

I switch back to <Deb>.

```
<Deb> Ssssssh, By-tor, if Ma hears you she
  will kill you.
```

I switch back to <Ma>.

```
<Ma> Who's under the bed, Deb?
```

I switch back to <Deb>.

```
<Deb> No one, Ma. I was reading the Bible.
<By-tor> eats some soap
<Deb> Ohmigod, Ma has the belt!
<By-tor> runs
<Deb> Swack! Swack! Swack!
<By-tor> streaks from the room, naked.
<Deb> Swack! Swack! Swack!
*** <By-tor> parts channel #Lovechild
```

I don't really blame him for leaving in such a rush. Frankly, I was amazed that young <By-tor> stuck around as long as he did.

Personally, I was having a wonderful time, but I'm not sure I would compare it to sex.

Perhaps I was not compliant enough.

Here, in any case, is what I think this episode reveals:

1) Male cybersex partners don't care how obviously sarcastic the female becomes, because they are just too lust-driven to notice, and

2) I would probably have made a very histrionic female.

I don't really know why <By-tor> put up with all of my silliness and smart-aleck remarks. Perhaps he thought I was just living out my sexual fantasy.

Perhaps I was.

I will get professional help soon.

But I have done it now, Mr. Thoreau. I have lived deep and sucked all the marrow of cyberlife. I have experienced cybersex, and you have, too, I suppose, by proxy. I didn't like it much, as a replacement for sex, but it did make me giggle.

A fair number of people, though, such as Martha, seem to like it quite a bit.

Why? Well, the most obvious answer would be safety. Net sex is the ultimate in safe sex, and I don't just mean safety from HIV and other transmitted diseases. Net sex leaves us safe from commitment, from entanglement, from having others witness our embarrassment. Sure, there are weirdos, but they are thousands of electronic miles away, they can't hurt us. They can't even see us, they can only type words, and words are easy to ignore.

If we choose to talk about sex on the Net, or even engage in a sort of sex, we can do it without fear. No one really knows who we are, no one but ourselves needs to know that we are doing it, and if anything goes wrong, if an affair turns ugly or inconvenient, we can just switch it off. The perfect answer in a society that is increasingly busy, and increasingly unsafe.

Easy in, easy out, no regrets in the morning.

I have seen the future.

I already miss the past.

chapter twelve

BIG BROTHER AND THE BAD BOYS

The Dark Side of the Net

I had hoped to meet and interview some youngsters, ask them how they used the Net. I had even begun swapping messages and trading introductory questions with a few advanced techno-teens, but the interviews didn't work out. The kids just disappeared suddenly, because their parents didn't want them to talk with me.

Yes, I explained to the parents that I was writing a book. Yes, I named the publisher, offered to send references and phone numbers, but the parents (apparently) didn't believe me, because the previously friendly and enthusiastic youngsters just stopped writing back.

And do you know why?

Pedophilia.

There is a dark side to the Net, you see, and my journey cannot end without touching on that subject as well. There is some truth, and much hysteria, surrounding the many claims of digital darkness, and especially the notion that pedophiles roam the Net in search of young prey.

On-line child abusers are the bogeymen of the electronic age, profiled on tabloid television, chronicled in *Time, Newsweek,* and *USA Today.* A columnist for the *Seattle Times* was so upset by the supposed level of electronic child abuse that he even suggested it was "time to pull the plug on the Internet."

Well, is it true? Have pedophiles used computer networks to find young boys?

In a word, yes.

Is the danger exaggerated?

Greatly.

But it happens. In Chelmsford, Massachusetts, John Rex, Jr., was arrested and charged with using his own computer forum, the County Morgue, to recruit teenage boys. He is alleged to have asked one of these boys to help him kidnap an even younger boy, and the teenager instead tipped off the cops. Smart kid. A similar case came up in Cupertino, California, when a man using the Net name "HeadShaver" allegedly carried on a series of electronic mail conversations with a young boy, then convinced the boy to meet him in person, and subsequently kidnapped the youth and subjected him to systematic abuse.

The Florida Department of Law Enforcement has released a list of warning signs to help parents detect their child's possible involvement with Internet weirdos and pornography. According to the department, parents should worry if: 1) the screen goes blank whenever Mom walks into the room, 2) the kid uses vast numbers of diskettes to retrieve material, or 3) the kid tends to hide these diskettes under the bed.

Though the actual cases of on-line child stalking are few, parents, and police, have begun to take notice. Computer networks provide anonymity and easy access to lonely kids, and computer stalking by private E-mail is very difficult to prevent. "The electronic frontier is a beat without end," one California detective complains. "There are lots of criminals, but few cops." And to make matters worse, most police stations have fairly unsophisticated computer equipment, and most cops do not have the programming sophistication needed to catch their crooks.

But crime is crime, these sorts of crimes are surely among the most vile, and almost everyone on the Net would abhor such activity. Where things get a bit more sticky is when issues of free speech conflict with electronic community standards.

Remember, one trait that distinguishes Net people, the BBS and Usenet people particularly, is a pure belief in freedom of speech. Net people celebrate free speech. They are passionate about free speech. The Net *is* free speech, some will tell you. On the Net, you can say whatever you want, whenever you want, and distribute it to the world with the push of a button. The rich and the powerful have no special sway in Net circles. The major newspapers and television networks may be owned and controlled by (pick one: bleeding-heart liberals; conservative rich businessmen), but the Net is still essentially owned by no one, no one decides what is news and what is not, and no one censors the letters to the editor. Freedom of the press is said to belong to the person who owns one, and now millions of us, in effect, do.

When unpopular political opinions are expressed in Usenet groups, Net people usually applaud and point and say, "See, it's working." When someone started the first alt.sex group, the Net people said, "Sure, why not?" When alt.sex.fetish.feet was formed, people said, "Yes, of course, this is freedom!" Though some people worried that the raunchy alt.sex.bondage group might give conservative government censors an excuse to clamp down on the Net, no one really tried too hard to stop it. "Who are we to say what others should do in their private lives?" was the general attitude. "I may not like bondage, but I'll die for your right to talk about it!" Libertarians are a particularly active group on the Net.

And then along came NAMBLA.

NAMBLA is the North American Man Boy Love Association, a group that openly advocates the elimination of all age-of-consent laws. NAMBLA fiercely supports the right to consensual sex between children and adults, especially men and boys. NAMBLA makes the hair on the back of most people's necks stand up. And NAMBLA wanted its own Usenet group. NAMBLA wanted to talk about man-boy love.

Man oh boy, did the fur ever fly!

There is a group called alt.config where ideas for new groups are proposed and discussed, and if I had a nickel for every time the words "weird, sicko, disgusting, and repugnant" were aimed at the individuals attempting to start the alt.sex.pedophilia group, I would have many nickels indeed. Many, many nickels.

It was fascinating to watch the process. NAMBLA made even the most staunch defenders of freedom squirm with an acute case of the free-speech willies. It was a riveting test of the Netters' resolve. As the NAMBLA people and other pedophilia proponents accurately pointed out, they were not proposing to have man-boy relations, which remain illegal, on the Usenet group; they were just going to talk about man-boy relations and discuss the rightness of the laws, and just talking about the rightness of a particular law is certainly not illegal.

This was a compelling argument, and the free-speech Netters found themselves triply horrified—they were horrified to see themselves cast as hypocrites, shutting down someone's right to talk about something; they were, in many cases, horrified by NAMBLA and by the whole concept of man-boy sex; and they were horrified by the publicity that might be generated, in particular by the potential response of Senator Jesse Helms if they approved the group alt.sex.pedophilia.

How are groups approved or disapproved? This, like so much else on the Net, is a bit complicated. Groups are proposed, votes are solicited, the big guys who operate the big machines decide to add a new group or not. But there are ways around this, especially in the alt. grouping, and often the group formation process resembles chaos more than order.

Ultimately, anyone with a good computer who knows the correct programming codes can start an alt. group with or without the Net community's approval, and this is what eventually happened. The group was started with no clear consensus on its right to exist. The compromise was to call it alt.sex.intergen, as in intergenerational, as in one generation reaching out to another. And pigs can fly.

The Congressional hearings on all of this have not yet begun.

"It is amazing how many creatures live wild and free though secret in the woods." Oops, I just quoted Thoreau again. The man has got under my skin. I can't seem to shake that picture of him in my bedroom, holding the dead otter.

But yes, as I went deeper and deeper into the electronic forest in search of answers to my basic questions—Who is using this Net? What are they using it for?—I, too, was amazed by the creatures I found lurking in the dark corners.

There is a Usenet group called alt.shenanigans, for instance, where bad boys (and some girls) trade ideas and advice and gloat over their latest practical jokes.

For instance, under the heading "A GREAT Way to Get Even With a Bad Teacher Person," a really funny guy explained how he and his buddies went out to their teacher's driveway at three A.M. in the middle of a January snowstorm and cemented concrete cinderblocks to his driveway. The snow was three feet deep by morning, so the teacher never saw the cement blocks until the rear bumper had been ripped from his car. Hardy, har, har! If any of this is true, and it may not be, the bad teacher person missed about a week of work and sustained five hundred dollars worth of damage to his automobile. The person posting this shenanigan made it clear that the teacher "lived with his mother . . . [and] deserved everything he got for this one reason."

Oh, to be young again!

Another suggested shenanigan was to get access to the electronic mail account of some "loser," either by learning the loser's password or by waiting until the loser walked away from his logged-in college computer lab terminal to go to the bathroom. Then, ha ha, you could "compose an E-mail letter threatening to kill the President." Excuse me while I hold my side! To be fair, the author of this shenanigan advised that the message not be sent to whitehouse.gov, but back to the loser with some misleading information attached, so that the loser only *thought* that the message had been sent to whitehouse.gov. Then, it was suggested, you could forge an electronic message that looked as if it came from the Secret Service, and threaten the loser with arrest. Then stand back. Watch the loser wet his pants.

There are roving bands of anarchist hooligans as well, wandering from Usenet group to Usenet group, the most famous ensemble being alt.syntax.tactical, a group known for stirring up artificial flame wars. A flame war is when I flame you, you flame me back, I flame you again, others jump in to flame both of us for wasting too much time and too many words on flaming, we flame them for having the audacity to complain, and so on and so forth.

Here is what alt.syntax.tactical, or "a.s.t" for short, will do to incite mayhem:

First, they find a friendly, congenial newsgroup full of affable people who post politely and respectably. Then one or two a.s.t types join the group as secret agents, ask polite questions, get themselves known. Then, in what the a.s.t. guidelines call Wave One, other a.s.t. members post a flame to the group, or more likely, flame bait, something so controversial that people cannot help but get upset. The original secret agents respond with flames and counterflames, others are quickly drawn in, and pretty soon the majority of postings on the previously quiet and affable group revolve around flames, attacks, people calling for the attacks to stop, name calling, and accusations. The a.s.t. guidelines define success as the point when "the Majority or ALL threads in invaded newsgroup were started by us."

This was done in rec.pets.cats, for instance. Someone posted an absurd but seemingly sincere message to the cat lovers' group discussing the practice of stimulating his cat's vagina "with a Q-tip" to induce ovulation, so that the cat would not inconveniently and vociferously go into heat when he had a girlfriend over for dinner. He also complained that his second cat had particularly foul-smelling bowel movements. Some of the more earnest cat lovers offered calm advice, but suddenly hordes of previously unheard cat lovers appeared on rec.pet.cats and began suggesting horrible alternatives, like putting the kitties in the microwave, nailing them to the wall, shooting them in the head.

The real cat lovers were understandably unnerved, and began posting messages to counteract this inexplicable tidal wave of anticat activity. The a.s.t. types, of course, then began attacking the true cat lovers, accusing them of all sorts of crimes and indiscretions, and for a short while nearly all the sensible people left rec.pet.cats.

I have witnessed other newsgroup invasions of this sort, and frankly, they are sort of fun to watch, assuming one of your favorite groups is not the victim. But it is rude, sophomoric, and does little to promote the idea that the Internet will raise mankind to some kinder, gentler level of consciousness.

Then there are the hatemongerers. One fellow spent the first half of 1994 literally flooding the Internet with long messages that began "SHOCKING NEWS: There Was No Holocaust" or "HOLOCAUST HOAX: Six Million Jews Never Died." He posted his vitriolic garbage hundreds of times, to hundreds of groups: the world history groups, of course, the Jewish culture groups, but also to the auto repair groups, and the cooking groups, and everywhere else. People tried to stop him, but how? No one knew who he was.

Nor was he the only one. Matters got bad enough that Rabbi Abraham Cooper, associate dean of the Simon Weisenthal Center, a group that investigates and exposes neo-Nazis, complained, "It may be time for the FCC to place a cop on the Superhighway."

The April 1995 terrorist bombing of the Oklahoma City federal building triggered further calls for Net anarchy to be more closely monitored. Did the bombers use the Internet to communicate their plans? This suggestion was made within days of the bombing, but no one offered evidence. Is information on bomb making available on the Net? Yes, but the information has been around for years in books and pamphlets. Is there incendiary talk and hate propaganda on the Net, in Usenet groups like misc.activism.militia and alt.politics.white.power? Yes again, but in the wake of renewed calls for Internet regulation following the Oklahoma bombing, Net defenders were quick to point out that our national security might be better served by clamping down on libraries, shortwave radios, G. Gordon Liddy, and mail-order publishing houses. For that matter, what about the national telephone system, which is also used by potential anarchists? Or what about rental trucks?

There are homophobes, racists, and misogynists on the Net, and the anonymity of it all seems to give them a dizzying feeling of freedom. Posting hateful attack messages on Usenet groups is a bit like spraying graffiti on a public wall, but in the case of Usenet postings, there is little chance of being caught, and it probably isn't even illegal. A coward's dream.

Is there more of this hate talk on the Net than in "real life"? No, probably a little less, but it's easier to find by accident and in ways it can seem more repulsive. While the sensible among us would never invite a rabid anti-semite into our home to spout his malicious rubbish or spraypaint our dining room wall, with Internet connectivity, the wires that link every computer to every other computer, the anti-Semite's message might just appear some evening on our "personal" computer, in our family room maybe, in our most private spaces. This can be disconcerting; it can make us feel violated.

Bad boys, bad boys. There are so many of them, it is hard to keep track. Impostors are all over the Net. Men posing as women. Women as men. Kids as adults. Adults as kids. I joked once on a book discussion group that I, in fact, was Stephen King, and pretty soon this kid in New Jersey started flooding my mailbox with fan mail. He was "so excited" to know my electronic address and wanted my opinions on all my books. But I was only kidding!

Newsweek, on the other hand, reports that an unidentified record label was caught hiring paid shills to talk up new bands on the progressive music groups, trying to create an artificial groundswell of popular support and thus sell more records. There will always be snake oil salesmen, it is only the product that changes.

For the moment at least, until a secure system of encryption is worked out, many experts advise that you should never give your credit card number out to anyone on the Internet. They may not be who they claim to be, or perhaps they are, but someone else may have found some sneaky way to intercept their mail and steal your card number. Many people are now working on a secure system for Internet mail-order, but my advice is to wait until they finish, test it, and prove that it is secure.

By the way, this illustrates one other potentially dangerous aspect of Internet life—your electronic mailbox is not so wonderfully secure, either. To enter my ATM machine and steal twenty dollars, you would need my password *and* my card, but to read my electronic mail or send false mail under my name, all you would need is my password. Back in the 1994 Winter Olympics, when Tonya Harding was the center of the world's imagination, three American reporters were caught reading the figure skater's E-mail, though they denied finding anything of interest. Her password was on her plastic Olympic Village ID card, she wore that card on a chain around her neck, and someone took a photo, blew it up, and read the numbers. There are electronic means of learning someone's password as well, though I don't claim to understand them. There have been computer hackers as long as there have been computers, and you should never underestimate the resourcefulness of a hacker.

With all of this bad-boy activity going on, you may ask, Where are the Net Cops?

Well, remember, there is the problem of jurisdiction. No single entity owns the Net. It is made up of an ever-growing number of separate networks voluntarily joining forces in a vast cooperative effort. No one can really set enforceable rules. That is why Usenet, for instance, seems like anarchy. It *is* anarchy, of a sort. The Internet has been hailed as "the largest functioning anarchy in the history of the world." Lots of people continue to post suggestions for good Net citizenship, but no one can make you follow them.

Only if what is being done is a crime can conventional crime-stoppers step in, but this gets very complicated, too. Regular hometown cops are responsible for stopping computer child abuse and other forms of stalking. If you engage in securities fraud on the Net, that is a matter for the federal regulatory authorities. If you threaten the president, expect a visit from men in dark suits with sunglasses. If you attempt to sell drugs, maybe the DEA will catch wind. But no one agency, or enforcement group, patrols the Internet. No one is really in charge.

It is not even clear if the United States government has jurisdiction. Sure, much of the Internet was built by American government funding and by American universities, and the vast majority of users right now are American, but the Net crosses a number of international boundaries. Think of it as air space, international air space, and no one national government can regulate international air space. Maybe the UN can form a commission to look into this. Maybe we will all be dead before the commission agrees on the shape of the table.

Eventually, though, most realists agree that the U.S. government will have to find some way of regulating what happens, at least within its borders. Based on current statistics, it seems likely the Net will continue to grow like a weed, and in addition to E-mail, Usenet, IRC, all of that, the Net will become a main source for on-line library catalogs, airline reservation systems, electronic shopping linkages, and the much-touted five hundred channels of cable television. Something this big, the argument goes, is just too important for the federal regulators to ignore.

And if those predictions come true, the Net may very well become victim of its own success. So many people will want to use this tremendous new information resource that the current Internet infrastructure will not be able to handle all the traffic, and someone will have to step in to build a newer, bigger, better one.

Who will it be?

Greedy, self-serving big business monopolists? Or free-speech libertarians with no intent to control or profit?

Don't make me laugh.

I asked my highly placed House sources about this, and they said without hesitation that we Americans should expect full corporate involvement somewhere not too far down the pike. Communications companies like AT&T and Sprint already own part of the Net's "backbone."

"Building the Information Superhighway that Vice President Gore is talking about is going to require money," my sources pointed out, grinning, "and the only way to get money is to get these people to build it."

So here is the scenario—a conglomerate that includes a merger of Time-Warner, QVC, Beatrice Foods, Microsoft, and Disney builds this new network—shining, gleaming, interactive, with fiber optic cables running into every living room—and for a reasonable fee they provide all the programs, all the channels, all the commercials, and allow us to shop from the convenience of our BarcaLoungers; and they, of course, have access to demographic profiles of our shopping preferences as well as our medical records, perhaps, and our educational records—certainly our preference in computer discussion groups. They know how much electronic mail we send, and to whom we send it. The software exists even now for them to search every bit of our electronic mail for key words and phrases (such as "I am a sex pervert" or "I plan to buy a new car next month.") They know just about everything there is to know about us, more than we know about ourselves.

And what will they do with all of this information?

If you are just a little bit skeptical, maybe even paranoid, the answer is obvious.

Target marketing!

They will use this inside knowledge of our buying habits to drive us so deeply into debt that our grandchildren will be born already owing this Time-Warner-QVC-Beatrice-Microsoft-Disney aggregation every cent they will ever earn.

Oh, brother!

Oh, Big Big Brother!!

George Orwell may have been right after all. He was just off by a few short years.

chapter thirteen

And If Your Head Has Somehow Not Yet Exploded, Let Me Briefly Discuss the Future

The Web and Other Wonders

When this book finally comes out, I am sure to receive a dizzying burst of angry flames from people who don't like my approach. With any luck, the good folks on alt.culture.internet will actually rise as one to condemn my efforts. "He spends all his damn time talking about E-mail and Usenet," they will complain. "Why the hell doesn't he talk more about anonymous file transfer protocol? What is he, some sort of thick-headed, untutored moron?"

Putting that last question aside for the moment, let me point out that "anonymous file transfer protocol" is simply impossible to say three times real fast. It is also, undeniably, a part of the Internet, as are Archie searches, Gopher servers, and telnet connectors to remote hosts. These tools are available, they are useful, but their operation tends to be technical. They are used most often by those people who must do research as part of their job or college education. In most cases, the use of ftp, Archie, Gopher, and the like requires patience and a distinct idea of what information is being sought.

So flame me if you must. I have telnetted to remote hosts, executed Archie searches, grazed through many a Gopher menu, and what I found was a zillion megabytes of information, most of it intended for highly computer-literate academics and software engineers. It is useful information, surely, but mostly to a select cadre of professionals.

The World Wide Web, however, is another story entirely. I promised in the first chapter not to dwell on predictions and prognostication, and though I lapsed a bit in the chapter just previous, I have pretty well kept to that pledge.

Now, though, let me look slightly forward to the World Wide Web. It is accessible right now, though only to Net users who have a sophisticated and usually more expensive Net connection called Slip or PPP, and access to a program such as Mosaic or Netscape; yet it is so utterly flashy, fun, and user-friendly that it is bound to catch on.

In computerese, the World Wide Web (or WWW) is known as a graphical interface. Graphical as in graphics, meaning pictures—photographs, even short snippets of jerky video, and big colorful typefaces. This, in and of itself, is an amazing revelation to anyone who has spent hours, days, weeks, and months staring at nothing but orange letters on a black screen. The World Wide Web, however, is also what is known as a browser. It has hypertext links.

Hypertext links?

Sounds like electronic sausage, and in a way, it is. Though the workings are fairly technical, the beauty of the World Wide Web is that it is not at all complicated to use. Just as somebody once suggested that the common man might do well to never witness how sausage is made, the common Web user would probably do best to ignore the complex code that drives a hypertext link. Just press the button, and watch it work.

How *does* it work?

Let's say you are reading a short item on your computer screen, a discussion of aliens from outer space, and you are drawn to the question of whether these aliens are likely to have webbed feet. Let us pretend that this document has been made available to Web readers by researchers from some esteemed university in Sweden. When you run across the words "webbed feet" in the text, you notice that the words are highlighted in blue, so you use your mouse (the computer pointing device, not the rodent) to put the cursor arrow on "webbed feet," and you click the mouse key. With absolutely no further effort on your part, a picture of green webbed feet appears on the screen, with the caption "What They Might Look Like." You enjoy this picture for as long as you like, perhaps gather your young ones around the computer to see it as well, then go back to the text, and read further along that "Investigators at Louisiana State University's Alien Lifeform Applied Research Lab have studied the alien landscape data and have mathematically determined that webbing is far more likely than a conventional sequestered toe configuration." Fascinated by this, as anyone would be, you click on this portion of the text, and the World Wide Web software does all the work necessary to lift you out of the Swedish research document and into a separate document housed on a mainframe computer thousands of miles away, deep in bayou country, and your screen blinks again to reveal the original Louisiana State study on alien toe configuration. You read that document thoroughly, click a certain phrase, and you are then instantly linked to yet another document, this one from Duke University, a study suggesting that the aliens are not even green but blue, and look like little devils, and a portion of that document might mention Al Gore, the vice president, and his views on alien podiatry, and if you click his name your computer might jump again to a document housed on a computer in Washington, and maybe you will even get to see a picture of the veep in a suit and tie.

Well, I made that up so you could see how it all works, but the truth is I did find a picture of Al Gore on the World Wide Web, in fact I found it within two minutes. It was my very first day using the Web, so I initially went to a document explaining the World Wide Web itself, and in talking about the Information Superhighway, the document mentioned the vice president. I clicked on Al Gore's name to see what would happen, and the photo shortly thereafter filled my screen. The VP was in his shirtsleeves, squinting into the sun, with just the hint of a smirk on his lips. Gore seemed pretty darn pleased with himself in that picture, and why not? He may very well go down in history as founder of the Information Superhighway, or at the very least as the guy who coined the name.

And by the way, I found webbed feet, too. Not on Al Gore, of course, but in a graphic and graphical hypertext document called the Interactive Frog Dissection Tutorial, made available to

Web browsers everywhere by the University of Virginia. I read about frogs, about the various layers of a frog's anatomy, and I saw many frog pictures, even a nice shot of the foot, which looked alien enough to me. In a section called Internal Organs I clicked on the word "spleen" and saw large close-up color photos of the spleen, with and without the liver folded back. This was more of the frog's spleen than I really needed to see. And I watched a dissection in jerky, fuzzy computer video.

That was fun, but not fun enough, so I went next to a document (of a kind that Web people sometimes call "home pages") titled "Gateway to Antarctica," and found, in page upon page linked to other pages, all I ever wanted to know about the history of the frozen continent, about its geological formation, about the birds and ferns and seals, and after clicking a few times, I ended up in the Antarctica Gift Shop. Yes, really. "It is fair to say that Antarctica is the last great continent," I read on my screen, "and, for most of us, it is beyond reach. But now, with items from this catalogue, we can all share in the wonders of Antarctica."

Nothing is beyond reach, it seems, on the World Wide Web, but I passed on the I VISITED GONDAWANALAND T-shirts and went instead to the home page of the Department of the Interior's U.S. Geological Survey, got bored within a hypersecond, then clicked over to NASA's Goddard Space Flight Center and found many Shoemaker-Levy comet impact photos and nothing at all about alien feet. I went next to the home page of the Missouri Botanical Garden to bone up on North American flora, then skipped up to Canada for something called Carasso's Home Page ("Think of this not so much as a Web page as a cry for help," it instructed) where I found links to various Web documents that could help me improve my bowling score, pass a drug test, learn to belly dance, and become rich by working part-time at home. And this home page even allowed me to view photos of Michael Jackson's wedding to Elvis Presley's daughter, and around then my head started to really hurt.

If you have ever oscillated your TV remote control back and forth between CNN Headline News and the Weather Channel while half-listening to NPR's "All Things Considered" on the radio and simultaneously chatting on the phone with a guy named Tony and answering questions from your six-year-old daughter, you know how I was beginning to feel. My head was a balloon about to burst, because all the information in the world is a wonderful thing, but I can only use so much of it. I had finally achieved true overload.

So I stopped.

I reached over and turned off the machine.

I went outside in the bright sunshine and stared into the sky.

I looked for flying saucers.

None came, so I can't tell you if alien feet are actually webbed, but the Internet is webbed quite nicely, thank you, and the Web goes World Wide.

The Web is just another doily, but this one actually weaves itself together. Though most home computers don't yet have the hardware and software needed to make full use of the Web, and though actually receiving all these data-intensive pictures can be excruciatingly slow, you can count on the tech wizards to solve these problems eventually, and when they do, the World Wide Web may very well be the future of the Net.

The Web is a sort of cross between television and Usenet, you see, and as someone who has found himself addicted to both at various stages of his life, let me say right now that the World Wide Web is pure info-tainment.

Who needs five hundred channels of television when the WWW has thousands of channels up and running already? The Web makes your mouse nothing more than a high-tech remote control channel-changer, and really, what single technological innovation of the past twenty years has caught on bigger than the remote control?

"There is more day to dawn," Thoreau notes near the end of *Walden,* and who am I to disagree? These electronic woods are only beginning to take shape, and there will be surprises, surely, along with the new growth. Wanting to hike a little further, curious to see just a bit more of the future forest, I contacted current Web users, asked them where they thought all of this was headed.

Web users tend to be younger, more hip to the trends, cynical and innovative at the same time, and the answers that streamed back ranged from "this new technology will someday save the world" to "it's all coming to a crashing halt in about twelve months."

The most thoughtful response came from Great Britain, from Christian Darkin, a twenty-six-year-old comedy scriptwriter, BBC radio reporter, and computer journalist. He uses the Web, he says, because he is "curious about everything," and he predicts there will be plenty of changes down the road, changes none of us can foresee.

"I think the Web is part of a process of development which started with scent-marking our territories and picking fleas off each other," Darkin writes. "The history of the human race from the very start has been about finding better and better ways to work together." He traces our development from hunting groups, to tribes, to villages, to nations, and finally to on-line global communities. "It seems that this progression leads us inevitably towards 'ultimate connectivity,' the state of total communication between all humanity which world leaders, hippies, religions, and talk show hosts have been talking about since we learned to speak."

I liked the sound of Darkin's words but wondered if I was being misled by clever cybergibberish, the tangled mesh of jargon and futurespeak so common on the Internet. I wrote him back the next morning, my E-mail skimming across the Atlantic in mere seconds, and asked for clarification. Was "ultimate connectivity" just a buzz phrase, or did it mean something?

"Think about it," Darkin responds. "One of our main drives as human beings is our curiosity. We need to learn. To explore. But we are limited in this by our physical bodies. I may want to learn about the furthest galaxies, I may have the mental capacity to understand the information I seek, but I cannot fly. I cannot see far enough, travel fast enough, or live long enough to gain the knowledge. So I build machines. Technology extends my senses, increases my strength. It allows me to narrow the gap between the potential of my mind, and the potential of my body."

Communicating by computer, Darkin goes on to say, is just another technology to extend our senses, to transcend our bodies and experience what would otherwise be physically impossible. When we trade words between my home in the U.S. and his in Great Britain, we are leaving our bodies behind, meeting through other means.

"But," he adds, "in order to communicate with you, my brain works my thoughts into words, then sends electrical signals into my muscles to move my fingers across the keyboard. Now, if I could somehow interrupt that flow of electrical signals from the brain, and send it to a computer, so that instead of controlling a real body in the real world, I was controlling a virtual body on the Internet, I could move, touch, hear, and see the electronic world just as I do the real one—effectively I would be there. There would be no limitations. I could have as many limbs as my mind could control. I could add on senses whenever I needed them.

"This is all quite beyond our current technology, of course, but not by so very far. It just requires better electronics, and a better understanding of neurology, and few would dispute the speed at which these fields are moving."

Those fields *are* moving fast, as is the field of computer networking, and Darkin's imagination is not exactly sluggish. He goes on just a little further—the future may be stranger yet.

"If I can become a part of the network," he concludes, "use its functions as my muscles, and its databases as my memories, and other people around the globe can do the same, then it stands to reason that I could—with permission—share their memories, see the world through their eyes, borrow their skills, and they mine. That is what I mean when I use the phrase 'ultimate connectivity.' It may seem farfetched, but if minds can be connected in the same way as computers, and there is no reason to think that they cannot be, each part retaining its individuality but at the same time becoming part of an infinitely more powerful organism, then we will have reached the state that religion, art, politics, and evolution have been promising for centuries. That is, a species of one mind, understanding all, and seeing all."

Time will tell, but it is an interesting vision, and Darkin is not the only one making predictions along these lines. Understanding all, and seeing all, may be somewhere in my future, in all of our futures, and that will be something indeed.

For the moment, though, I'm still trying to simply understand how my modem works, what exactly we are supposed to be discussing on the Usenet newsgroup alt.bitch.pork, who is going to regulate this Information Superhighway eventually, and whether they are just going to ruin it.

Oh, and one other thing. Do aliens actually have webbed feet?

Maybe someday the Internet can teach me that.

chapter fourteen

BACK TO NATURE

The Concluding Chapter

The woods are lovely, dark, and deep, and yes, they are becoming very, very crowded. But are they useful?

Is this electronic lace doily something transcendental, transformational, consequential, or profound? Will it really change who we are?

John Perry Barlow, founder of the Electronic Frontier Foundation, the Net's main lobbying voice in Washington, has no doubt at all. "When I first got a sense of the Net," he writes, "I went around saying that it would have a greater consequence on what it is to be human than movable type. I am now inclined to think this is the most transforming technological event since the capture of fire."

Excuse me while I wipe the hyperbole off my glasses. Did it just get a bit thick in here?

Okay, it is Barlow's job to exaggerate, maybe, but he is not alone in his euphoric revelation. Idealistic thoughts of this sort crowd the Net and much of the attendant media coverage. The Internet, in some strained, bloodshot eyes, is not a mere technological marvel, but a religion. We will all, soon enough, find ourselves wired in, connected, interlaced, sipping at the holy font of digital knowledge, feeding on electrons rather than diet pretzels, and in this way we will be transformed, as Christian Darkin colorfully predicts, into one vast human mind, one giant human soul, one enormous, harmonious being.

If you've read any science fiction, you know where the idea comes from, but science fiction is fiction, and the Internet is real.

I spent my year in the woods, raking up those leaves of jargon, fishing for truth in the pond of the electronic culture (even surfing a bit), and warming my hands by the virtual bonfire called Usenet, but I'm afraid my conclusions are a bit less dramatic.

Will the Internet revolutionize planetary culture, transform global politics, rearrange the balance of world power? I looked for evidence, but I didn't find much. Sure, there are changes along the margin, some interesting changes, but as much as they might deserve it, I just don't see the old institutions tumbling down any time soon. If I were a dissident in Faroffawoola and had a computer, a modem, and total Net access, I would be thankful, and I would be very, very careful. My ability to communicate through an electronic network would help my cause, perhaps, but my problems would not be solved.

Is the American democracy, then, on the verge of some critical, evolutionary, Internet-inspired transformation? Will the entrenched Washington bureaucracy and the unrepresentative representatives go away with the push of a button that allows us all to vote at home, by computer, having our say on every bill, every amendment, every last federal initiative? Well, to be honest, I didn't find that either. Imperfect as it is, there is logic behind the idea of representative democracy, and the only way to really budge Washington would be if we all showed up one morning with our yellow bulldozers. And even then, who would get the federal contract to rebuild? Someone has to decide.

And what about those frightening, apocalyptic predictions of imminent doom? Will the Net lead to a new era of international sabotage? Yes, I suppose it will, because there will always be spies, and spooks, and counterspooks. Some of these slimeballs are perhaps breaking into Pentagon computers at this very moment, finding the dirty pictures some bored programmer stored on a corner of the hard disk. And maybe they are also finding plans to build a better bomb, or maybe they are finding the fake plans to build a better bomb planted by subterfuge experts at the CIA. Or maybe they are just finding that all the phone lines are busy, and their modems won't connect.

Are we headed toward a world filled with anemic drones laboring away at sterile keyboards, never taking a moment to sniff the ragweed, never twisting an ankle while tossing a frisbee to their flea-ridden dogs? Well, we might be. America, at least, has been headed there for some time, roughly since the invention of the fluorescent tube. The Internet, though, is just a symptom of our technological cocoonery, not the root cause.

I searched the electronic woods for all of these enormous, world-shattering, status-quo-upsetting changes. I looked and looked until my eyeballs would no longer focus, but I just didn't find proof. Instead of vastly altering our world, what I found was that the Internet and all its clever bells and whistles are rapidly being assimilated *into* our world.

Just look at the uses the American government has found for the Net: more press releases, more transcripts of speeches, more form letters to constituents, more smoke, more mirrors, more of the same. Or check out the infomercials that are beginning to crowd the World Wide Web, such as the Antarctica Gift Shop and Pizza Hut's electronic order desk. Yes, the Net gives every citizen a vehicle to discuss global affairs, religion, existential thought, but the most popular Usenet groups still rant on about petty politics, lurid sex, and prime-time television.

Will the arrival of vast electronic networks change the fundamental way we relate as human beings? I doubt that, as well, especially the "fundamental" part. But it was here, at least, that I found the most potential. Falling in love by E-mail is not so different from trading inked notes, but it does tend to whittle down the distance. The support one finds in on-line support groups is not so different from the comfort available at your local church, men's group, or AA meeting, but it is more convenient, safer, and thus taken advantage of more readily. Electronic communities like the Cellar and the WELL are an efficient way for busy people to stay connected, at least intellectually, to other busy people. And my ability to trade gardening tips with folks in the Netherlands will probably give me pause should a U.S. president ever suggest we annihilate them with a nuclear bomb.

Will cybersex ever replace the real thing?

God, I hope not, and having tried both, I would be very surprised.

. . .

So what *are* the implications?

The plan, according to a consensus of experts in telecommunications, the computer industry, and cable networks, as well as Al Gore himself, is that every home will eventually be wired and ready, every single American (and some day the world) will have access to this amazing resource, and this access will make our lives fuller, richer, easier, more wonderful somehow.

Will it? Probably not.

Listen to Thoreau again: "Our inventions are wont to be pretty toys, which distract our attention from serious things. They are but improved means to an unimproved end."

He is right, of course. An "improved means to an unimproved end" simply gets us where we were going anyway, though maybe a bit more quickly. Therein lies the central fallacy of the Information Superhighway. We are talking about a machine here: a pretty interesting one, but basically a big machine that spits data across long distances. Despite what varied sorts of machines we have at our disposal, despite all the uploads and downloads and listservers in the world, we are still going to be the same human beings, the same contentious, territorial, ridiculous, lovely, procrastinating souls. Net users love to crow that they are "connected," but to what? To the Net, of course; but ultimately we are just connected to one another, and that doesn't make us any different, it just means we are more in touch.

Wherever the human race is headed—and I'm not sure where that is—the Net may get us there faster, but we are still headed the same way. The electronic culture won't change the content of our lives, it will simply change the pace. We will all soon be swaying as one to the same quick Al Gore rhythm.

Can we just turn away, on the other hand, ignore the coming of the Net, cover our ears to the incredible traffic noise and belching smoke of the approaching Superhighway?

Thoreau tried that. He went off into his own woods, lived the simple life, tuned himself into the slow cycles of nature, ate his nuts and berries, shut himself off from all that was changing. Yet he didn't stay, did he? He eventually came back out and published his book.

Escaping the progress of mankind, ignoring the inevitable forward movement, is a common enough fantasy, but not much of a reality. The simple fact exists, this *is* our future.

But don't worry, it is probably not so bad.

How will we use the Net, the Web, the electronic lace doily, when it eventually weaves itself into every primitive home?

We will use it for entertainment, surely; increasingly we will use it for convenience; perhaps the day will come when we will *have* to use it for business. Eventually it will be integrated into the general infrastructure of government and commerce, and we will barely remember the day it wasn't there. Think of the telephone. Or for that matter, television. We are hard-pressed to exist without them, but did they ultimately change the world? Not that much, I think. Not in any fundamental way.

• • •

And as for myself, having spent these past twelve months hiking deep into the Internet forest, how did I survive?

Quite nicely, thank you.

But my head hurts, my eyes ache, and there are mornings when I think one more speck of vital information, one more fascinating tidbit of Usenet data, might just detonate my brain. Tempting as it is, no one needs to know everything.

Thoreau devotes an entire chapter of *Walden* to his occasional visitors, those brave people who tramped through the mud to sit in one of his three chairs, to nestle in his tiny cabin, those times when he and his guests "stand very near together, cheek by jowl, and feel each other's breath." My own friends sometimes stand too close, their breath can sometimes stink of stale coffee and smoke, some of them have stubbled cheeks and others have crooked jowls, but right now I greatly miss them. What I really want to do is meet these friends at a back booth of some Thai restaurant, eat platter upon platter of pungent food, shout across the table, and share all that's on our minds without the benefit of first thinking. I want to find the homeliest of these friends, the one most given to popping off half-cocked, the one who reeks the most of garlic, and I want to give the guy a hug.

A big hug. A real hug. With real arms.

The virtual world is virtually awesome, but it is only a virtual world, a reflection. I yearn for the real world, with all its torpid shortcomings.

The Information Superhighway is indeed big, fast, and dizzying, and if there is somewhere you want to reach quickly, it beats the living hell out of side alleys, service roads, secondary boule-vards, and city streets. But right now, frankly, I just want to park my car awhile.

Drive out to a real forest, park my car, step outside, and take a good long look at the scenery.

I love the scenery.

I love the way it holds so still.

AN INTERNET JARGON HANDBOOK

access provider

If you want to use the Internet, and you don't have free access at work or at school, you will need to pay someone—either a company such as America Online, Prodigy, or CompuServe, or one of the smaller, local access providers—to give you an account. Then you can access the Net through their big machines.

account

This is what you get from an access provider. In the case of commercial providers, it allows them to keep track of how many hours you spend logged on. It also allows an access provider to keep track of who you are.

address

In order to receive E-mail, you need an electronic address, something along the lines of yourname@accessprovider.com or president@whitehouse.gov.

Archie

A funny-looking redheaded guy in a comic book, but also a sophisticated search tool that will allow you to find files anywhere on the Internet by entering a key word. Once you locate the file, you will probably use **ftp** (see below) to retrieve it.

ARPANET

The Internet's grandfather, started in 1969, and named for ARPA, the Department of Defense's Advanced Research Project Agency.

auto-responder

A form of "bot," or robot computer program. If you send electronic mail to certain addresses, whitehouse.gov for instance, your message is automatically answered by a computer. The answer is just an electronic form letter, and your mail may or may not eventually reach human eyes.

BBS

Short for "bulletin board system," a computer-based mechanism that allows people to read other people's messages on their computers, and then post responses. No thumbtacks needed.

binary

A file that contains information other than just text. It is usually a program or a picture of some sort. Watch your kids closely.

bounce

Depending on your access provider's software, it might be

possible to adjust your settings so that incoming E-mail from certain outside addresses simply bounces off your mailbox. If someone has been repeatedly trying to sell you Herbal Weight Loss Remedies, for instance, this can be very helpful.

byte

Computer storage capacity—the amount of space your computer has to hold information—is measured in bytes. In the Net world, the more bytes you can handle, the bigger the dog you are.

cancel-bot

In response to **spamming** (see below), sophisticated programs called cancel-bots have been developed to robotically cancel certain messages from Usenet newsgroups. Since no one is officially in charge of Usenet, cancel-bot operators tend to be self-appointed, and many people object to their tactics. Others, having been offered an Herbal Weight Loss Remedy for the nineteenth time in two weeks, just say, "Thank you very kindly, cancel-bot."

channel

If you enter a Chat program, you will need to choose a channel. You can then chat with the other people who have also chosen that channel, assuming you have something to say to a total stranger.

Chat

The Internet and many of the larger commercial access

providers offer Chat areas, also called forums, where people can converse on-line in real time. This means that your typed messages appear on the screens of other users only moments after you type them in.

coding

Another term for programming—the act of writing logical instructions coded into computer language.

command-line interface

When you turn on your computer or dial into your Internet access provider, a command-line interface is what you see on your screen. It will often look like this:

```
>
```

or this:

```
=====>
```

And you will need to type in a command (such as "Menu"). The alternative to a command-line interface is the "friendlier" **Graphic User Interface** (see below).

crossposting

On Usenet, crossposting is the act of sending your article or message to two or more of the ten thousand different subject discussion newsgroups. Crossposting to more than one or two topic areas, especially if the relevance of your message is not clear, is considered rude. Crossposting to fifty or more groups tends to fire up the cancel-botters.

cybersex

Sex without touching, sex without seeing, sex with very little sensory input other than the clicking of hard plastic keys. Some people love it.

cyberspace

A term coined by author William Gibson in his sci-fi novel *Neuromancer.* People on the Internet argue all the time about what it means, or whether it means anything at all, but generally it refers to the geographically nonexistent space where computer-aided communication takes place.

download

Retrieving a file by yanking it from another computer "down" to your computer (see **upload**).

electronic mail (E-mail)

Messages sent from one individual across the Internet to another specific individual or group of individuals.

emoticon

Typed messages can be cold and sterile, so people have begun to attach little sideways smiley faces, like this :-) to indicate that they are being good humored, or winking faces ;-) to indicate that they are just joshing, or maybe this face #:*(to indicate a bad haircut and nasal congestion.

encryption

A type of software that will automatically transform electronic messages into coded messages, so other people can't read them. The intended recipient needs to use a software "key" to decode the message.

FAQ

Short for "frequently asked questions." You will find a FAQ file posted on many of the more active Usenet newsgroups, and before broadcasting your beginning questions across the group, you should probably read this first to see if your question has already been answered.

Fidonet

A worldwide network of bulletin board systems.

flame

Nasty, often obscene, messages traded by E-mail or Usenet posting. Some people flame others when they disagree with them, while others do it for fun. It is hard, though, for even the best of flames, aimed in your direction, to hurt much more than your feelings.

flame war

Nyah, nyah, nyah, nyah, nyah. Occurs when some people on Usenet just get childish and flame back and forth until everyone gets bored and begs them to stop.

freenet

Certain localities, Cleveland for instance, offer free on-line access for residents. Usually, though, you can't do as much on these services as you can on those for which you have to pay a monthly fee.

ftp

This means file transfer protocol, the way in which files are transferred from one computer to another. If you need information on some subject, and relevant articles are housed on a computer in Finland, you can ftp to that computer and retrieve them.

GIF

Short for Graphics Interchange Format, it is exactly that, a format by which to exchange graphic (i.e., picture) files.

gigabyte

Lots and lots of bytes (1,073,741,824, to be exact).

Gopher

An extremely useful area of the Internet that lets you find a wide range of information by browsing menus and then reading data files with no more effort than hitting the enter button on your keyboard.

graphics

Pictures, charts, maps. Beyond words.

GUI

Short for Graphic User Interface. On America Online, for instance, you will see pictures on your computer screen and can then point your mouse at those pictures to execute various commands. This is much easier for most people than remembering and typing in the proper sequence of words or letters, but it can slow down a system as well.

hacker

In the old days, there was always a guy who couldn't stop fiddling with his '57 Chevy. Nowadays, there are people (but still mostly guys) who can't stop fiddling with their computers, their software, their phone lines, and they can do some amazing stuff.

home page

On the World Wide Web, users set up what is called a home page, and by accessing that home page you can find out lots of neat stuff about the user, and then use hypertext links to jump to other related Web sites.

host computer

Most individual users can't connect directly to the Internet. Instead, they connect to a host (a college computer, a commercial provider such as CompuServe, a local access provider), and that host is their gateway to the greater Net.

hypertext

It looks like writing, but when you point to certain words with your computer mouse, amazing things happen. Not unlike a secret passage hidden in a Victorian library.

Information Superhighway

Everyone really in the know knows there really is no such thing. But it sounds big and exciting and like something the government should pour lots of dollars into, so the metaphor survives.

Internet

A network is two or more computers linked together. The Internet is made up of thousands of these networks, all networked together, to create one gigantic international Network of Networks. It is the closest thing to an Information Superhighway that we have today.

IRC

Internet Relay Chat, the Internet's chat zone, and a popular hangout for bored college kids.

Jughead

Yet another search tool that allows you to do keyword searches within Gopherspace. See also: **Archie, Veronica,** Mr. Weatherbee.

listserver (or LISTSERV)

Automated programs that manage mailing lists. Mailing lists are much like Usenet newsgroups, only the individual articles are E-mailed directly to a subscriber's mailbox.

log on

When you connect your computer to a BBS or an access

provider, you will usually need to type in your username and password. This is known as logging on. (Note to Star Trek fans: this really has nothing to do with William Shatner's *Captain's Log*, but you can certainly pretend.)

lurking

If you read the messages in a Usenet newsgroup but don't immediately add your own two cents worth, you have more self-control than I have, and you are what Internet types call a lurker. If eventually you decide to participate in the discussion, you are de-lurking. Some people lurk both ways.

mainframe

A big computer, many times more powerful than the one in your family room.

mailing lists

See **listserver**.

megabyte

Not as much as a gigabyte, but still a lot of bytes (1,048,576 actually).

modem

A piece of equipment you buy from a computer store, without which your computer can't call other computers and chat on the phone. Be a sport! Let your computer have a social life.

MOO

This is what cows say when you ask them, "Do you have E-mail?" It is also an acronym for MUD-Object-Oriented, which is a type of interactive computer game.

mouse

It sits alongside your computer on a mouse pad, and you move it around to move the arrow on your screen. Kids love them, typists hate them, and they are rapidly becoming indispensable.

MUD

Multi-User Dungeon, another type of on-line computer game, with roots in the old Dungeons & Dragons subculture. A MUD is more violent than a MUSH, and you may need hip-boots. (See also **MOO**.)

MUSH

Yet another interactive game, and an acronym for Multi-User Shared Hallucination. When I was in college, those words meant something else, but I never inhaled.

Net

There is the Internet, and then there are services such as America Online, Delphi, and CompuServe that might be linked to the Internet but are actually separate networks, and there is Usenet, Fidonet, and the various BBSs, and everyone will jump on your back if you use one of these terms incorrectly. So just say Net.

netiquette

Proper Net etiquette. Don't ask questions that are in the FAQ, don't SHOUT, don't quote personal E-mail without permission, and whatever you do, don't stick bubblegum under the virtual chairs.

newbie

Often preceded by the word "clueless," a newbie is a newcomer who hasn't learned Net rules or Net terminology. But we are all newbies at one time or another, and they should be welcomed.

newsgroup

Within Usenet, there are ten thousand newsgroups, divided by topic area. Check news.announce.newgroups for an up-to-date listing.

off-line

The opposite of on-line, of course. With certain software, you can retrieve your E-mail messages or collect a series of newsgroup articles on-line, then go off-line to read them and compose your responses. This is an efficient way to cut costs if your access provider charges by the hour.

on-line

Linked up, connected. When your modem dials into your access provider, and the connection is made, you are on-line. Being on-line is much cooler than not being on-line—just ask Al Gore or Newt Gingrich.

on-line service

Another name for access provider.

post

When you send your message (sometimes called an article) to Usenet, you are posting. Posting is the electronic equivalent of stapling your garage sale notice to a telephone pole.

queue

When someone sends you E-mail, it waits in your mailbox, in what is called a queue, until you come on-line and check your incoming mail.

real time

As opposed to virtual, or computer time, real time refers to the "now" of human time. When you're trading messages in real time, it's like you're on the telephone, or a two-way radio.

RL

Short for "real life." Some people find that they enjoy computer interaction so much, they forget to go outside. They never see real people. They get very glassy in the eyes. They need to be reminded about RL.

slip or PPP

A bit technical, but suffice it to say that this type of connection allows your computer to link directly into the Internet instead of merely piggybacking on some big host computer's Internet link.

smiley

See **emoticon**. Or don't, see if I care. :-)

spam

A message that is repeated and repeated and repeated to numerous Usenet newsgroups. The name comes from an old Monty Python routine, the one in the restaurant where someone orders, "Spam, Spam, Spam, Spam, Spam, Spam, Spam, Spam, Spam, Spam, and eggs."

spoof mail

An electronic wolf in sheep's clothing. Mail that doesn't really come from the indicated source.

system administrator

For most every access provider, educational site, or industry site, there is someone in charge. If you have a problem or complaint, find this person.

telnet

A program that lets you log on to other computers from afar. MOOs, MUDs, and MUSHes run this way.

threads

Within Usenet, certain topics can be discussed for weeks, or months. Such a topic is known as a thread.

UNIX

A computer operating system prevalent on the Internet. Crude but powerful.

upload

Taking a file that resides on your home or office computer and transmitting it to someone else's computer (see **download**).

Usenet

The Internet bulletin board system where you will find ten thousand newsgroups, one on each and every subject imaginable.

Veronica

Like Archie, another program with which to hunt down information within Gopher.

virtual

A buzzword that may or may not mean anything. Basically, if something exists in real life, if you can touch it, if it gets wet during a heavy rainstorm, it is real. If this something only exists in a computer somewhere, if it only happens on-line, it is probably virtual.

Virtual Community

People who know one another primarily through writing messages back and forth by computer, rather than by actually having met. Howard Rheingold wrote the book on this subject, *The Virtual Community*.

World Wide Web (WWW)

The newest thing, a hypertext system that lets you jump from document to document, with color and pictures. Very flashy, very cool, often very slow, and not all machines can run it, but for the moment, having Web access is an essential component of being totally hip. The only thing better is webbed feet.